T0294858

FINANCIAL FUNDAMENTALS FOR HISTORIC HOUSE MUSEUMS

FINANCIAL FUNDAMENTALS FOR HISTORIC HOUSE MUSEUMS

Rebekah Beaulieu

ROWMAN & LITTLEFIELD
Lanham • Boulder • New York • London

Published by Rowman & Littlefield
A wholly owned subsidiary of The Rowman & Littlefield Publishing Group, Inc.
4501 Forbes Boulevard, Suite 200, Lanham, Maryland 20706
www.rowman.com

Unit A, Whitacre Mews, 26–34 Stannary Street, London SE11 4AB

British Library Cataloguing in Publication Information Available

Library of Congress Cataloging-in-Publication Data

Names: Beaulieu, Rebekah, author.
Title: Financial fundamentals for historic house museums / Rebekah Beaulieu.
Description: Lanham : Rowman & Littlefield, 2017. | Includes bibliographical
    references and index.
Identifiers: LCCN 2017023094 (print) | LCCN 2017028204 (ebook) | ISBN
    9781538100325 (Electronic) | ISBN 9781538100301 (cloth : alk. paper) | ISBN
    9781538100318 (pbk. : alk. paper)
Subjects: LCSH: Historic house museums—Finance. | Historic house
    museums—Accounting. | Historic house museums—Planning.
Classification: LCC E159 (ebook) | LCC E159 .B36 2017 (print) | DDC
    907.4—dc23
LC record available at https://lccn.loc.gov/2017023094

Printed in the United States of America

Contents

Preface

You love historic house museums, right? You feel a thrill as you duck to enter the front door through a slightly undersized frame, enjoy the creak of centuries' old floorboards as they arch slightly to accommodate your weight. The surfaces might be slightly dusty; in the air there's a particularly cozy scent of old wood, a tinge of cleaning product, and age. While activities like educational programs for kids or group tours may buzz around you, you move through historic structures as you do through libraries and other sacred spaces: slowly, quietly, and with great care to disturb nothing around you. You revere the materiality of the history that surrounds you, the tangibility of the past, and the welcome disorientation of finding yourself transported in time.

And at some point, something happened that brought you to here. You accumulated enough of those experiences visiting sites to consider joining the fledgling board of a new historical society. Or you became passionate about a historic house in your neighborhood that was slated for demolition, and banded together with other residents to save the house with the idea to open it as a museum. Perhaps you are a recent graduate of a museum studies or art history program, who always appreciated historic sites but never imagined working for one—and the rare paid museum position offered to you happened to be in a historic site. Maybe you recently retired and thought volunteering in the small history museum in your local community would be a great way to spend your time and give back, never realizing how much the overworked administrator desperately needs an extra pair of hands.

This book is for all of you: for everyone who has, stirred by their passion for the museum field and for history, found themselves to be in a position of responsibility for a historic site. It is intended to be a helping hand, a guide, and an essential reference as you build a historic site that is for public education and engagement from a property. This book accommodates readers of all levels and in a variety of positions in historic sites, and offers insights into the financial needs particular to historical organizations.

A 2014 article in the *Boston Globe* titled "The Great Historic House Museum Debate" by Ruth Graham quotes Stephanie Meeks, president of the National Trust for Historic Preservation, as saying that most historic house museums are financially unsustainable and require better and more creative financial management to survive. "The time for talk has ended," she announced, "and the time for action is upon us."[1]

This book is the response to that call for action and is a timely contribution to the field. Since Richard Moe, Meeks's predecessor as president of the National Trust, published his provocative essay "Are There Too Many Historic House Museums?" in 2002, the history museum sector of the museum field has received intense scrutiny into their ability to build sustainable operations.[2] The scarce scholarship dedicated to historic house museums continues to fall squarely into two camps, as they have for the past twenty years: the work of historic preservation, or interpretation and visitor engagement (or both). Available texts offer discussions of general management needs, such as placing ads for housekeepers and how to outsource all financial management; others attend to the pragmatic needs of preservation practice. Other publications focus on interpretation, collections, and contested histories. And those texts that focus on professional topics in historic house museums often deal with finance tangentially, their dedication remaining firmly rooted in audience development or more general administration.

But how do we, as site professionals, get to the point of debating the relevance of our tour narratives? How do we find ourselves in a position in which our greatest concern is visitor engagement? What we need to recognize, to understand, and to embrace is that after a house has been "saved" from private ownership or demolition, it must be managed well to welcome visitors in the first place. The board, staff, volunteers, or some combination thereof must weather the first year of operation as a museum by establishing effective, strategic, and compliant methods by which to oversee the operation with finance in mind. This book essentially demystifies the financial business of historic houses. Unique in both content and perspective, it fills a void in museum administration literature that is vital to the viability of historic house museums in the United States.

This text is designed to serve this fundamental purpose and is written for a variety of readers. Students in nonprofit management, museum studies, material culture, and art history who may be considering cultural site management can benefit from the introduction to basic financial management concepts. Similarly, educators in such programs may find use in the accessibility of this text. Preservation professionals—not simply staff but also board members, volunteers, and anyone else who works in site management—may learn about financial systems. This publication is for those who contribute their time and service to historic sites like house museums, but may have no formal training in accounting or experience in managing institutional finances.

This book is *not* for accountants, business managers, or financial analysts. If you are trained in any of those field and are interested in working in historic house museums, hooray! Welcome! We need you! Your expertise will be embraced. That said, this might not be the crash course you need. I should also mention that while certain segments of this text, such as how to handle historic designation, might be of use to historic house museum owners, it is not designed for private residences that happen to be historic. There are plenty of resources, such as the National Trust for Historic Preservation, that can help with residential tax credits and other pertinent topics.

Instead, this book recognizes and tackles the most admittedly unappealing aspects of historic site management, perhaps the very subjects that many who are interested in history have avoided until now. Before we even get started, let me state something that may be obvious to me but not yet to you: I'm one of you. I'm a humanities-loving, liberal arts–educated, nose-in-a-book museum lover. I didn't grow up dreaming of spreadsheets and balanced budgets; I was too busy reading Louisa May Alcott and imagining undiscovered secret passages in my house. As I grew up and decided to dedicate my career to museums and took a special interest in historic house museums, I realized that there was a vast expanse of the historic house museum field that no one wanted to touch with a ten-foot pole: money. Whether we are soliciting donations, devising earned revenue options, or simply managing our resources, many people in the museum field are uncomfortable directly addressing the topic. Some may say that history buffs and museum people can't hack savvy management, and that's why many museums—historic sites particularly in the crosshairs—find themselves in lean or even financial circumstances.

I have more faith in us than that. I invested time to learn about finance, fiscal responsibility, and the language of numbers, and found the resultant knowledge to be invaluable and empowering. You can do the same thing. Whether it is the group of neighbors who saved the local dilapidated, Gilded Age–era mansion from the wrecking ball, or the historical society members who took over administration of a local landmark from their town, we history lovers are not scared of hard work or big projects, and we're not afraid to harness our collective energy to save treasures. Let's not forget that American preservation began with history lovers, enthusiasts, and those willing to roll up shirtsleeves, not those who had the perfect management pedigree. I'm pretty sure no one in the Mount Vernon Ladies Association piped up as they organized to preserve Mount Vernon and said, "Thank goodness I have my master's degree in architecture with a concentration in historic preservation practice and an MBA in nonprofit management!"

Much of the American preservation movement has been instigated by passion and dedication. We simply need to utilize that spirit and that commitment to create well-structured systems of operation for these sites, which often come unequipped with funds, staff, or any clue of what to do first, next, or last.

This book should help with the transition from a secured structure to a functioning museum. Other professional resources can offer guidance on general management topics such as human resources needs or risk management, but this is your go-to reference for finance. The primary aim is to provide enough basic information to provide understanding of the fundamental principles and needs of nonprofit financial operation. The enemies of passion and advocacy are fear and lack of information, and this text arms you with the knowledge to recycle the ambition and energy required in successful advocacy and preservation into stable financial oversight.

Each chapter of the book provides an accessible introduction to the financial necessities of a historic site and addresses the major financial activities you will undertake in a nonprofit organization. Chapter 1 details the steps needed to formally establish and incorporate your site, how to construct your mission, and how to think strategically as you take your first institutional steps. Chapter 2 offers instruction regarding contributed income and the different forms it may take, how to track donations, and how to properly acknowledge them. Chapter 3 focuses on earned revenue, a variety of typical revenue-generating activities, and how to effectively plan for and manage earned income. Chapter 4 discusses the structure of financial management in regard to budget building and financial tracking, presenting accounting procedures and standards. The fifth chapter is dedicated to forecasting and reporting income, and the IRS Form 990, including its completion and various uses in strategic short- and long-term strategic planning. Each chapter also includes a summary checklist of action items, as well as case studies of actual historic house museums currently in operation across the country. The sites documented capture a variety of scale and resources. You may find that some cases will resonate with issues you are currently facing, or may strike a chord at some point in the future for you at your site. Their purpose is to encourage you to learn about different methods of planning, tracking, and evaluation activities in the field, and to consider a variety of approaches to common issues.

The general trajectory of the text will guide you from initial incorporation, through activity management and documentation, and conclude with reporting and forecasting. You will learn, and most likely experience, the interdependent cycle of the different activities of the financial cycle, from planning through execution and, finally, evaluation.

To recognize the need to address the financial situation of your historic site and invest in broadening your knowledge basis is a great first step. You are already committing to the work necessary to create a sustainable historic site. Soon enough, you will be welcoming potential donors to cocktail parties, hosting school groups for tours, and mounting capital campaigns to restore the site to glory. But before you get there, you will want to enact structures and policies to ensure the foundling organization will function at a level of productivity, transparency, and solvency.

Look at it this way: Historic sites are one of the most unique forms of cultural organizations in the world thanks to their unequivocal ability to tell a story. Historic structures and properties are imbued with the history of the country, the culture, the people. When you formalize a historic place into a museum, you continue its story and write a whole new chapter. Your work of programs, events, and preservation and the people who experience it with you, whether they are board members, volunteers, or donors, revitalize a site. Narratives of the past life of a historic site are not the only stories to be told: the documentation of its current activities, priorities, and challenges recorded in organizational materials tell of its life in this moment. This story may be told in a new language of numbers, but consider this: we in the history and museum fields are natural storytellers. You're simply learning to speak a new language. Please allow me to serve as your translator.

Notes

1. Ruth Graham, "The Great Historic House Museum Debate," *Boston Globe*, August 10, 2014, https://www.bostonglobe.com/ideas/2014/08/09/the-great-historic-house-museum-debate/jzFwE9tvJdHDCXehIWqK4O/story.html.

2. Richard Moe, "Are There Too Many House Museums?" *Forum Journal* 16, no. 30 (Spring 2002): 4–11.

Acknowledgments

There are many people whose contributions have made this work better, stronger, and without whom this project simply would not have been possible. I wish to convey my deepest gratitude to Charles Harmon of Rowman & Littlefield, whose steady confidence and advisement was invaluable as I took this book concept from a nugget of an idea to a fully realized book in record time. I also wish to thank Michelle Beckett, editor extraordinaire, whose comments invariably make my writing stronger (and often make me laugh at the same time!).

I am grateful beyond words to my colleagues in the museum field who offered continuous support and welcome perspectives on the topics of museum management and historic sites throughout my writing process. We are an innovative, opinionated, and smart bunch of people, and I love working with you all. I particularly wish to thank those individuals who shared their time and expertise directly to the production of this publication. I offer my most sincere appreciation to the individuals interviewed for this book, whose candor and reflections are a vital component of this project and will, I'm sure, prove extremely worthwhile to readers: Michael Cogswell of the Louis Armstrong House Museum; Joshua Torrance of the Woodlawn Museums, Gardens and Park; Elizabeth Mowll Lay of Montgomery History; Rachel Abbott of the Minnesota Historical Society; Barbara Palmer, formerly of the Bidwell House Museum and now of Williams College; Gennifer Sauter of the Conrad Mansion; Rowena Dasch of the Neill-Cochran House Museum; Marta

Bones of the Pittock Mansion; and John Eastberg of the Captain Frederick Pabst Mansion, who served as an interview subject for earlier research on the mansion, in my dissertation. And speaking of my dissertation, of which this is an unexpected by-product, I wish to thank professors William Moore and Keith Morgan of Boston University, for their unwavering and unmatched guidance as I completed my dissertation on historic house museum management.

Finally, I would like to thank the individuals in my personal community who have bolstered both my confidence and my energy as I undertook the near-impossible tasks of completing this book while finishing a dissertation and working full time. I am so fortunate to work with a fantastic team at the Bowdoin College Museum of Art: my colleagues both within the museum and at the college as a whole comprise the best and most accomplished group of colleagues with whom I have had the pleasure to work. A special thanks to my family: my parents, Dan and Debbie Beaulieu, who knew I was going to write this book about fifteen years before I did; Jerome and Julie Ford, who have fostered a renewed appreciated of historic houses in the greater Chicago area just to keep me in the loop; and of course, to my husband, Patrick Ford. Marrying you was the smartest thing I ever did.

1

Building the Foundation

Organizational Structure and Incorporation

Imagine that you are a politician, in the midst of a campaign for election to office. You are working tirelessly, constantly sharing your message with your potential constituents, some of whom share different opinions and ideologies. You are single-minded in your dedication to your goal: election. And then, Election Day arrives . . . and you win! Amazing! You feel on top of the world! But then you wake up the next morning and think, *Holy cow, what comes next?!* I have to make good on all those promises I made, work with people who don't necessarily agree with my causes, and figure out how to make it all happen.

Preservation and the associated work of managing a historic site are like that. The achievement of the goal of saving a house from demolition, or transferring ownership from a developer, resident, or municipality can feel triumphant and empowering, dazzling in its potential and is similar to winning an election. Yet there is nothing conclusive about taking on a historic site, since this part of the journey is only beginning. What do you do the moment you transition from a preservation advocate to a site administrator or board member?

This chapter introduces the basic steps necessary to define your historic site as a mission-based organization and to undergo the legal process of proper incorporation. We will examine the creation of (1) your mission, which is your goal;

1

(2) your business and strategic plans, detailing how will you accomplish your goal; and (3) your incorporation, the structure under which you will achieve your goal.

Working through the steps outlined in this chapter will undoubtedly make your site a stronger organization and will help your board and staff to be more prepared to maneuver the legal and financial minefields that can deter many from realizing their dream of turning a historic house into a museum. And speaking of board: before you establish any organizational activities, make sure you have assembled a group of people willing to serve as the inaugural board of the site. The size of your board should be of a manageable size as you start out, perhaps no more than ten individuals. Your board members should be able to offer their time and expertise whenever relevant, whether to the operation of the site, community outreach, or potential fundraising. This group of people will be the nucleus of activity and thought as you begin operation.[1]

By tackling this necessary and integral work as you initiate a project with tangible benefits to your community and its history, you are doing everything you possibly can to ensure its successful future. Let's cross the threshold (pun fully intended) to making a historic museum together.

Defining Your Mission

Before all else, I recommend drafting a working mission statement. This statement may change over time, but your mission should always function as a succinct summary of your purpose and the definition of your work. Your mission statement will be a necessary component of every form you submit in support of incorporation, every application for funding you draft, and every document you make public. Its utility is broad, but its composition should be clear and straightforward, answering the following questions:

- Who are you (your organization)?
- What are you doing?
- In what ways are you accomplishing your purpose?

Essentially, your mission is a well-prepared elevator speech. While you may agonize over the exact wording of your mission statement, you want to keep it simple and easily understood. Here are some sample statements:

From the Mount Vernon Ladies' Association that oversees the Virginia home of George Washington, Mount Vernon:

> This mission of the Mount Vernon Ladies' Association is to preserve, restore, and manage the estate of George Washington to the highest standards and to educate visitors and people throughout the world about the life and legacies of George Washington, so that his example of character and leadership will continue to inform and inspire future generations.[2]

The mission statement of the McFaddin-Ward House, a 1905 Beaux-Arts Colonial house in Beaumont, Texas takes a different approach and provides a list of points:

- Preserve and interpret the McFaddin-Ward House, its collection, and the history of the family.
- Interpret the history of Southeast Texas including its architecture, materials, and aesthetic culture, agricultural and business interests, especially as they relate to the house, its collection, and the family, through tours, educational programs, publications, and exhibits.
- Cooperate with community groups involved with the promotion of historical and cultural activities, tourism and education.[3]

And the Historic Adamson House and Malibu Lagoon Museum, a 1929 Moorish Revival home in Malibu, California, provides a third example:

> To provide for the inspiration and education of our visitors through interpretive activities and to assist in the preservation of the Historic Adamson House. To protect the park's extraordinary biological diversity and its most valued natural and cultural resources. To maintain ongoing and updated information of said cultural and natural history pertaining to all aspects of the Museum and House. To assist financially through fundraising activities in accomplishing the above objectives and purposes.[4]

These examples all highlight objectives related to the history and community they serve. They differ in format and specificity, yet they are each explicit in their dedication to their goal of preservation and its relation to public service, which is vital to a good mission statement.

While your mission statement is the invaluable cornerstone of your organization, you want to build into your plans the opportunity to revise the mission. Perhaps your site will be the recipient of a large archive of materials, or you will grow the physical property to include adjacent historic buildings. There are a number of valid reasons to update mission statements, as long as such revisions are handled thoroughly and with foresight, since all organizational documents will reflect such changes.

Also worth mentioning is that you are not limited to your mission statement as the sole tenet of organizational direction. Other planning documents that are complementary to the mission statement include the vision statement (the statement of objectives and their relation to organizational potential) and the statement of values (the statement of core beliefs guiding operational activities). These documents are optional, and I recommend you draft a mission statement first, which will surely realize ideas better suited to potential vision or values documents (or both). Use these draft documents throughout your initial planning phase, and return to them often to sharpen your statements.

Business Plan and Strategic Plan

Concurrent with defining your mission, you should make time for strategic and business planning. These are two different processes and should not be confused. Your strategic plan details the "how and when" of your organization. Consider it the map by which you chart the course of your entire operation, its priorities, and goals. A strategic plan will shift over time as the composition of your board changes, the community needs shift, and financial or programmatic needs dictate, and future strategic planning will be rooted in analysis of past activity and reevaluation of the strategic plan in place. In the creation of your first strategic plan, there exists the freedom of a clean slate. Stick to basics and answer questions that will result in a structure to guide initial activity:

- What are your goals? (This language should reflect your mission statement.)
- What steps do you need to take to reach these goals, who will do them, and what resources are needed for their successful completion?
- How will you measure success?

Along with you mission statement, your strategic plan is an essential planning document as you get started. Many grant agencies, such as the Institute of Library and Museum Services, require a strategic plan to be included in funding applications. It also serves as a supporting document for incorporation. Your strategic plan should function as a guide by which funding is sought, programming is determined, and operations are stabilized. Furthermore, there should be few situations in which any organizational decisions deviate from the strategic plan or mission; consider both to be components of a guide to consistently follow. That is not to say that you cannot seize unexpected opportunities as they arise, but your strategic plan should provide fundamental criteria as to whether or not to embrace such options.

The strategic plan works hand in hand with the business plan.

Your business plan is the "who and what" of your operation, the functional process by which you expect to accomplish your goals. You want to answer the following questions:

- Who are the key players in this organization and what value do they contribute?
- What makes this organization different from the competition?

- Who is your audience, what do they want or need, and how will you reach them?
- What financial activities will we undertake to meet our goals?

A business plan is of greatest use in the beginning phase, which is probably the point at which you currently find yourself. Unlike the strategic plan, which must be reviewed and updated at regular intervals, the business plan is more of an internal work plan after the initial phase of organization. Together, your mission, strategic plan, and business plan fully document your objectives, your purpose, and how you plan to reach your goals. Every organization is responsible for answering these questions—whether it's a historic house museum or a billion-dollar for-profit enterprise—and thoughtful responses should provide the information necessary to complete incorporation.

Incorporation

Once you have completed your mission statement, strategic plan, and business plan, you will want to formally incorporate the museum. Incorporation is the legal process by which you form any organization. The procedure of incorporation consists of filing a series of forms with state and federal governments in order to receive official recognition as an entity with its own rights and obligations. A word of advice: while I advocate for tackling as much of this internally as possible, it is advisable to connect with a lawyer for matters relating to incorporation. At this point, I would strongly recommend at least having the contact information on hand for when you have particular questions, which will come up as you execute the next few steps.

To create your organizations, you will need to draft your articles of incorporation and bylaws, a series of documents with the Internal Revenue Service (IRS), and potential additional documents with the state. Let's go through each, one by one:

Articles of Incorporation

Articles of incorporation, also referred to as "articles of association" or "certificate of incorporation" (the term varies by state), is the name most commonly given to the document that functions as the initial declaration of your organization (see figure 1.1). The IRS provides sample language to assist you in the writing of your articles.[5]

The purpose of the articles of incorporation is to create the entity, and to establish the organization's purpose and dissolution clauses. The IRS essentially needs to determine if you intend to function for public service. Your purpose should include your mission statement, followed by standardized clauses that should be included in your articles verbatim:

> Purpose: The organization is organized exclusively for charitable, religious, educational, and scientific purposes, including, for such purposes, the making of distributions to organizations that qualify as exempt organizations under section 501(c)(3) of the Internal Revenue Code, or the corresponding section of any future federal tax code.[6]

> Dissolution: Upon the dissolution of the corporation, assets shall be distributed for one or more exempt purposes within the meaning of section 501(c)(3) of the Internal Revenue Code, or the corresponding section of any future federal tax code, or shall be distributed to the federal government, or to a state or local government, for a public purpose.[7]

As long as you follow the guidelines offered by the IRS and include the language above, your articles of incorporation will serve as your organizational document for legal purposes.

Bylaws

While the articles of incorporation serve to formally create your organization, your bylaws are equally important as the guiding document for governance and functional purposes. To put this in terms of American history 101, the articles of incorporation are your Declaration of Independence and your bylaws are your Constitution. Your bylaws should be clear, concise, and should address at least the following:

Figure 1.1. IRS Articles of Incorporation.

Articles of Incorporation of ____. The undersigned, a majority of whom are citizens of the United States, desiring to form a Non-Profit Corporation under the Non-Profit Corporation Law of ___, do hereby certify:

First: The name of the Corporation shall be ____.

Second: The place in this state where the principal office of the Corporation is to be located is the City of ____, ____ County.

Third: Said corporation is organized exclusively for charitable, religious, educational, and scientific purposes, including, for such purposes, the making of distributions to organizations that qualify as exempt organizations under section 501(c)(3) of the Internal Revenue Code, or the corresponding section of any future federal tax code.

Fourth: The names and addresses of the persons who are the initial trustees of the corporation are as follows:
Name _____ Address _____

Fifth: No part of the net earnings of the corporation shall inure to the benefit of, or be distributable to its members, trustees, officers, or other private persons, except that the corporation shall be authorized and empowered to pay reasonable compensation for services rendered and to make payments and distributions in furtherance of the purposes set forth in Article Third hereof. No substantial part of the activities of the corporation shall be the carrying on of propaganda, or otherwise attempting to influence legislation, and the corporation shall not participate in, or intervene in (including the publishing or distribution of statements) any political campaign on behalf of or in opposition to any candidate for public office. Notwithstanding any other provision of these articles, the corporation shall not carry on any other activities not permitted to be carried on (a) by a corporation exempt from federal income tax under section 501(c)(3) of the Internal Revenue Code, or the corresponding section of any future federal tax code, or (b) by a corporation, contributions to which are deductible under section 170(c)(2) of the Internal Revenue Code, or the corresponding section of any future federal tax code.

(If reference to federal law in articles of incorporation imposes a limitation that is invalid in your state, you may wish to substitute the following for the last sentence of the preceding paragraph:

"Notwithstanding any other provision of these articles, this corporation shall not, except to an insubstantial degree, engage in any activities or exercise any powers that are not in furtherance of the purposes of this corporation.")

Sixth: Upon the dissolution of the corporation, assets shall be distributed for one or more exempt purposes within the meaning of section 501(c)(3) of the Internal Revenue Code, or the corresponding section of any future federal tax code, or shall be distributed to the federal government, or to a state or local government, for a public purpose. Any such assets not so disposed of shall be disposed of by a Court of Competent Jurisdiction of the county in which the principal office of the corporation is then located, exclusively for such purposes or to such organization or organizations, as said Court shall determine, which are organized and operated exclusively for such purposes.

In witness whereof, we have hereunto subscribed our names this ____ day of ____, 20__.

- the size of the board and how it will conduct business
- the general roles and responsibilities of board members
- rules for holding meetings, electing board members, and appointing officers
- the establishment of board committees
- rules of governance, including conflict of interest policies and the establishment of board terms of service
- any other essential matters of governance

Your bylaws may be amended in the future, but should remain the central document that articulates the governance structure and serves as the operating manual for the site. Public dissemination of your bylaws is not required, though it is a good idea to make them readily available to encourage transparency. Bylaws may, however, be required to be filed alongside your articles of incorporation; check your state's regulations to be sure.

After you have completed your articles of incorporation and bylaws, both documents should be signed and notarized. Your articles of association can usually be filed online, though you will want to check your state's procedures. The date the document is accepted by the state is generally considered your date of incorporation, though you may request a later effective date (useful if you aim to establish your organization at the start of a fiscal year). By the way, isn't it great when the IRS makes things easy for you? Well, hold on to that feeling, because more IRS filings lie ahead.

Documents for Tax Purposes

The IRS requires several documents to be filed in addition to your articles of incorporation:

- Application for Employer Identification Number (SS-4): The application for your Employer Identification Number (EIN) is commonly thought to be required only if you plan to hire employees, which is incorrect. This is actually your tax identification number and it will be required on all tax documents filed with the IRS, including those to follow in this chapter. Make sure to complete this after your articles of incorporation, but before you apply for tax exemption status, since it is required to complete the application. It is also necessary for all banking needs, such as opening accounts in the name of the organization. A handy chart accompanies the SS-4 to assist you in completing the form.
- Request for Tax Exemption: The application for federal tax exemption provides the acknowledgment of the legal entity for public benefit. Organizations classified as 501(c)(3) have a charitable purpose, and consist of public service, religious, and educational organizations. You will have to include your date of incorporation, which as you know, is the date on which the state processed your articles of incorporation.
- Power of Attorney and Declaration of Representative (2848) and/or Tax Information Authorization (8821): The IRS requires documentation of those authorized to access the financial records of the nonprofit organization, as well as those authorized to act on its behalf. Since you will want to authorize a lawyer or accountant to have access to such files, you will want to review both forms. Form 2848 allows the listed representative to "receive and inspect my confidential tax information and to perform acts that I can perform with respect to the tax matters listed." Form 8821 authorizes an appointee "to inspect and/or receive confidential tax information for the type of tax, forms, periods, and specific matters listed."

State Documents

You will also need to file a series of documents with your state to ensure legal recognition. These vary from state to state, but potential documents to file include the following:

- Name Reservation Request: Some states, like Georgia, offer the option of a name reservation request to be filed for the legal entity. See figure 1.2 for an example.[8]

  Other states, like California, offer a similar document that provides information on the name of the organization as well as contact information for the organization and key members, and the name of a fiscal agent. Often this process is elective, designed for you to protect and reserve your organizational name, especially as you undergo the process of drafting the articles of incorporation. Review your state's guidelines and have all information ready.

- State Charter: In some states, like New York, a charter is a required component of the organizational process and is similar to, and can even function as, the articles of incorporation. New York museums are chartered and governed under the New York State Education Department, and the charter serves two purposes: first, the charter delineates certain guidelines for the function of museums and historical sites within the state, and second, it involves the review of best practices in accordance with the American Association of State and Local History as well as the American Alliance of Museums. Figure 1.3 is a sample request for a provisional charter from New York.[9]

  As you can see, the language of the charter is very similar to that of the articles of incorporation recommended by the IRS, right down to the clauses regarding purpose and dissolution. Check with your state to see if a charter is required.

- Declaration of Trust: It is possible that your state will require a declaration of trust, for your organization will most likely be a trust if not a corporation. A declaration of trust is a statement by the title owner of a property that the property is being held for the benefit of another person or entity. This document basically records the anticipated relationship between an owner or property holder and the beneficiary. Perhaps a developer has purchased land that includes a historic site and is amenable to the site remaining and functioning as a historic site. The Metropolitan

Figure 1.2. Georgia Name Request.

Brian P. Kemp
Secretary of State

OFFICE OF SECRETARY OF STATE
CORPORATIONS DIVISION
2 Martin Luther King Jr. Dr. SE Suite 313 West Tower Atlanta, Georgia 30334 (404) 656-2817
sos.georgia.gov

NAME RESERVATION REQUEST

Applicant Name:

Street Address:

City: _____ **State:** _____ **Zip Code:**

Email Address:

Phone Number:

The nonrefundable filing fee is **$25.00**. The fee is for performing the search and will not be refunded if the name is not available. You may apply to reserve a name by completing this form and submitting it to our office with a check, cashier's check or money order made payable to the Georgia Secretary of State. You may also request a name reservation online at sos.georgia.gov. Online filers can pay using a credit card (M/C, Visa, Discover or AMEX). Once approved, you will receive a name reservation number valid for 30 days. **Within 30 days, you may file entity formation documents using the name reservation. Name reservations cannot be renewed and will expire after 30 days**. However, you may reserve the name again for $25.00 as long as the name is available.

If the requested name is not available a rejection notice will be sent via telephone, email or US mail. The notice will include instructions on submitting another request within 10 days of the notice without additional charge.

Please be advised that the online system only performs a preliminary search of our database. An in-house examiner will perform a detailed search and confirm whether or not your name is available. Your name is NOT confirmed and reserved until you receive official notification from this office.

No activity or investment under a name, such as advertising, purchase of a seal, entry into legal transactions, etc., should be conducted based on a name reservation. Such action should not be taken until the entity formation documents are filed and a certificate of incorporation, certificate of organization, certificate of limited partnership, or certificate of authority is issued by the Secretary of State.

Please indicate your choice(s) for a name: (Enter the exact name of the organization.)

♦ **1st preference:**

♦ **2nd preference:**

♦ **3rd preference:**

Please return this form, along with your payment to: Office of Secretary of State, Corporations Division, Name Reservation Request, 2 Martin Luther King Jr. Dr. SE, Suite 313 West Tower, Atlanta, Georgia 30334.

Waterworks Museum in Chestnut Hill, Massachusetts, functions under such a system: the museum, originally the Chestnut Hill Waterworks until the 1970s, is part of a parcel of land that was purchased by a developer who turned the property into condominiums. The Waterworks Museum operates under the Waterworks Preservation Trust, which outlines operational and financial expectations.

Other: Memorandum of Understanding

Don't hate me, but there is another legal document that is not required by federal or state government, but it is one that I consider to be vital to organizations. It's called the memorandum of understanding (MOU). In this case we are referring to a statement of permanence, but now includes such agreements as leases, management contracts, and other documents to outline the expectations between a steward organization and its beneficiary. For our purposes of historic site management, the MOU generally refers to any document that formalizes the relationship and mutual expectations between a parent organization—for profit or nonprofit, museum or otherwise—and your site.

Let's say you are in the process of designating a historic house adjacent to a college. A member of the administration of the college approaches you and offers to take ownership of the site, financial support, and to allow you to oversee operation of the property as a historic house museum. Sounds great, right? But then a year later, a new college president arrives, the administrator with whom you struck that deal is ousted, and there is no record of your arrangement. The new president isn't really a fan of the house, decides to reallocate funding, close the operation of the house, and simply consider the property an asset for tax purposes. Or worse: he decides the college needs a new administrative building and decides to raze the house altogether. What can you do?

If you have an MOU on file, you can fight back. If you are considering a relationship with a nonprofit parent steward, it

Figure 1.3.   Sample Charter.

PETITION FOR PROVISIONAL CHARTER

TO THE REGENTS OF THE UNIVERSITY OF THE STATE OF NEW YORK:

We the undersigned, all being persons of not less than eighteen years of age, desiring to form a corporation under the Education Law, do hereby apply to the Regents of The University of the State of New York for a provisional charter to be granted pursuant to the provisions of section 216 of such law, and do make, sign, and acknowledge the following statement:

First:　　　　The name of the proposed corporation is *(insert corporate name)*.

Second:　　　The purposes for which such corporation is to be formed are: *(list the planned activities of the proposed corporation, i.e., why it is being formed)*.

Third:　　　　The proposed corporation is to be a nonstock corporation organized and operated exclusively for educational purposes, and no part of the net earnings of the corporation shall inure to the benefit of any individual; and no officer, member, or employee of the corporation shall receive or be entitled to receive any pecuniary profit from the operations thereof, except reasonable compensation for services.

Fourth:　　　The institution to be maintained by the proposed corporation is to be located at *(street address, city or town, county--indicate if there is also a different mailing address)*.

Fifth:　　　　The number of trustees is to be not less than five nor more than twenty-five.

Sixth:　　　　The names and post office addresses of the first trustees are as follows: *(give names in full, including any middle initial; use a married woman's own first name rather than that of her husband)*.

Seventh:　　　The Commissioner of Education is designated as the representative of the corporation upon whom process in any action or proceeding against it may be served.

Eighth:　　　Notwithstanding any other provision of these articles, the corporation shall not carry on any other activities not permitted to be carried on (a) by a corporation exempt from Federal income tax under section 501(c)(3) of the Internal Revenue Code of 1986 (or the corresponding provision of any future Federal tax code) or by (b) by a corporation, contributions to which are deductible under section 170(c)(2) of the Internal Revenue Code of 1986 (or the corresponding provision of any future Federal tax code).

Ninth:　　　　No substantial part of the activities of the corporation shall be devoted to carrying on propaganda, or otherwise attempting to influence legislation, (except to the extent authorized by Internal Revenue Code section 501(h) as amended, or the corresponding provision of any future Federal tax code, during any fiscal year or years in which the corporation has chosen to utilize the benefits authorized by the statutory provision) and the corporation shall not participate in or intervene (including the publishing or distribution of statements) in any political campaign on behalf of, or in opposition to, any candidate for public office.

Tenth: Upon dissolution of the corporation, the board of trustees shall, after paying or making provision for the payment of all the liabilities of the corporation, dispose of the remaining assets of the corporation exclusively for one or more exempt purposes, within the meaning of section 501(c)(3) of the Internal Revenue Code of 1986 (or the corresponding provision of any future Federal tax code), or shall distribute the same to the Federal government, or to a state or local government, for a public purpose. Any such assets not so disposed of shall be disposed of by order of the Supreme Court of the State of New York in the judicial district where the principal office of the corporation is then located, exclusively for such purposes or to such organization or organizations, organized and operated exclusively for such purposes, as said Court shall determine.

In witness whereof, we have made, signed, and acknowledged this application on this day of _____, 20__.

(Signatures of at least five of the trustees listed in Article Six; may be signed in counterparts with separate notary acknowledgments. Any trustee [beyond the minimum of five] named in Article Six who does not sign the petition will not be named as an incorporator and must submit a separate, notarized consent to serve as an initial trustee.)

STATE OF NEW YORK)
ss.
COUNTY OF _____)

On this _____ day of _____, 20__, before me personally came (*insert names of all applicants who signed the petition*), to me known to be the persons described in and who executed the foregoing application, and they severally duly acknowledged to me that they executed the same.

(Typed name, stamp and signature of notary public)

---

benefits both you and the steward to draft an MOU to document your relationship. In such a document, you can clarify if your historic site will have its own board, how communication will be managed, and the funding structure, if relevant. Most important is the articulation of the purposes and protection of the structure itself and its collection. In our example, should the college face lean times, MOU documentation will be the shield that resists the sale of the historic property and its collection for income.

MOUs do not have to be extremely long, but they do need to enumerate the specifics of any arrangement and the protection of associated cultural assets. Include the following information if you need to draft an MOU:

- background and objectives: the purpose of the document
- statement of work: what the museum will provide (usually educational value and/or management of structure and collection), and that which is provided by the steward (financial support, facility resources, etc.)
- terms of agreement: including how often the MOU should be reviewed by representatives of the steward and beneficiary
- key parties: the representatives of the steward and beneficiary who will lead communications, as well as the system of reporting and documentation for personnel changes
- prior approval: a statement that nothing can be changed, deaccessioned, or destroyed without prior knowledge, and
- property utilization: important for historic structures, provides the language for the use of the building and collection, as well as site access and the potential for physical removal of the collection, which should be avoided as much as possible.

The National Park Service website offers language that can assist for such arrangements in their Property Management Regulations. For a general sample MOU, see figure 1.4 from the Nasher Museum at Duke University.[10]

As you can see, the MOU outlines the expectations for the beneficiary, in this case the Nasher Museum, as well as the steward, Duke University. The Nasher Museum MOU is a sample that the Association of Academic Museums and Galleries (AAMG) regularly recommends for guidance, though I would encourage historic sites to also make sure to include additional language regarding the preservation and educational value of the structure itself, not only the collections held within.

Historic Designations

The application for historic designation is a step that can fall anywhere in the process from well before incorporation to years into function as a public site. A *designation* is the status conferred to a site by a local, state, or federal agency that oversees preservation initiatives and documents sites of significance. A designated site is one that is listed on any local, regional, or national register of historic places. Perhaps the most well known of all registers is the National Register of Historic Places, which was developed in 1966 as part of the National Historic Preservation Act. Additional registries are maintained at the state and local levels.

The process of designation is absolutely worthwhile, though it is important to note what designation does and does not provide. Any designation nomination will require the inclusion of historic documents, photographs, and architectural assessments of the building. Therefore, it is most useful as a resource to your organization and to the general public. Additionally, many preservation-oriented grant-making agencies require certain designations, so the work of securing designations can serve an important funding purpose. No designation, however, protects a building from demolition. In fact, the only protection offered is against federally funded capital projects that would adversely affect the designated site. Do not assume that a designation ensures permanence, but consider it to be a valuable tool in terms of safety and proper maintenance.

National Register of Historic Places

Since local processes for specific designations vary, let's focus on the process to be listed in the National Register of Historic Places (NRHP). The best place to begin with the NRHP application is with your local historical commission. If your town does not

Figure 1.4. Statement of Permanence. Duke University

𝔇𝔲𝔨𝔢 𝔘𝔫𝔦𝔳𝔢𝔯𝔰𝔦𝔱𝔶
𝔇𝔲𝔯𝔥𝔞𝔪
𝔑𝔬𝔯𝔱𝔥 ℭ𝔞𝔯𝔬𝔩𝔦𝔫𝔞 27708-0030

OFFICE OF THE SECRETARY
217 ALLEN BUILDING

BOX 90030
TELEPHONE (919) 684-2641
FAX (919) 681-7657
secretary@duke.edu

RESOLUTION
NASHER MUSEUM OF ART

WHEREAS, the Duke University Museum of Art was established in 1969, and until 2005 was housed in a former science building on East Campus; and

WHEREAS, in 2005 the Nasher Museum of Art at Duke University (the "Nasher"), the successor to the Duke University Museum of Art, opened in a new facility on Campus Drive, and since its opening the Nasher has provided students, faculty, staff, alumni, and the larger Durham, regional and global community with all of the educational and cultural advantages offered by a world-class museum; and

WHEREAS, the University has provided and continues to provide both capital and operating support to the Nasher since its inception; and before that provided continuous support to the Duke University Museum of Art; and

WHEREAS, on the fifth anniversary of the opening of the Nasher it is appropriate for the University to recognize the important role of the Duke University Museum of Art in the intellectual and cultural history of the University, and at the same time recognize the current importance of the Nasher to the mission of the University as an intellectual and educational resource for the University, and re-state the commitments of the University to the Nasher;

NOW, THEREFORE, BE IT RESOLVED, that the Executive Committee Board of Trustees of Duke University does hereby:

1. recognize that the Nasher is an important division and integral part of Duke University;

2. recognize the importance and contributions of the Nasher to Duke University and its mission as an intellectual and educational resource, and applaud its many successes in its educational endeavours, exhibitions, community outreach, the public recognition of the superior status and reputation of its professional staff, and the continued enhancement of its collection;

3. express the commitment of Duke University and its resources to provide capital as well as operating support for the Nasher to ensure its continued success and the attainment its mission;

4. recognize the Nasher and its collections as essential components of the mission of the Nasher and not ordinary assets that are available to the University as disposable

assets; and

5. express a commitment to exercise its fiduciary obligation to protect the museum's assets, both tangible and intangible, and to fully support the Nasher in its compliance with the standards set forth by the American Association of Museums and the Association of Art Museum Directors including policies relating to collecting and gift acceptance, deaccession, and the use of deaccession proceeds.

Submitted to the Executive Committee of the Board of Trustees on June 18, 2010.

Approved by the Executive Committee of the Board of Trustees on June 18, 2010.

Signed: _____
Richard V. Riddell
Vice President and University Secretary

cc: P. Lange
R. McCaughan
K. Rorschach

---

have a local historical commission, contact your State Historic Preservation Office (SHPO). It is imperative that you contact an agency when you wish to embark on the application process because you must receive nomination to the register. A program officer will review your case and if he deems it worthy of inclusion on the NRHP, the officer will instruct you on assembly of the nomination packet. This application should include any relevant materials from public archives as well as private ones: was it the residence of someone who (or whose relatives) may have papers and photographs of the house? Did the structure once house a business that may have institutional records to offer? Keep in mind that you are creating the formal record of the site, and any materials you can record provide a benefit to you and to the public.

Once you have submitted the documents to the local or state office, they will be reviewed and you will be notified if the nomination to the NRHP has been made, or if more documentation is needed. Don't worry if they ask for more! The officer is there to make your nomination as strong as possible and can provide critical feedback. Your nomination will be evaluated according to its *significance*, and that is what you wish to highlight. NRHP listings usually fall into one (or more) of the following categories of significance: (1) architectural significance, which reflects excellence in an architectural type, period, method of construction, the work of a master, or that possesses high artistic value; (2) historic significance, a site that directly made a contribution to history or is likely to yield information about history; and (3) biographical significance, associated with a significant person. Documentation of such significance in one or more areas is necessary for a successful nomination.

The nomination form is a six-page document: the first page requires signatures and the remaining pages are for narrative text concerning significance. See figure 1.5 for a sample.[11]

National Historic Landmark

Confusion often arises over the difference between a site listed on the NRHP and one listed as a National Historic Landmark. They are actually quite different and their nomination processes diverge significantly.

The National Historic Landmark program falls under the 1935 Historic Sites Act, a completely different legislation than that which oversees the National Register. Its application is more rigorous, and national significance must be proven. Nominations are usually prepared as a result of a theme study, which links the site to an important theme or era of national history, such as the American Revolution or the civil rights movement. While a nomination to the National Register is handled by a federal agency, only the Secretary of the Interior can designate a historic landmark, of which there are only approximately 2,500 in existence. According to Jim Gabbert, Historian for the National Park Service, the NRHP process is from the ground up, and the Historic Landmarks program is from the top down.[12] If you are working with a property that you believe is worthy of landmark status, contact your state program officer for direction (though you may want to put it on the back burner until you have significant time to devote to the project). Regardless of what designation you seek, the case for preservation is one of the best forms of advocacy for its public prominence. Perhaps you have already undertaken such a step in the organization of your site and if you have, excellent—it can only help you in dealings with your community, municipality, and potential funders.

*   *   *

Case Study: The Captain Frederick Pabst Mansion
Milwaukee, Wisconsin

Mission: The Captain Frederick Pabst Mansion, Inc., a registered nonprofit organization located in Milwaukee, Wisconsin, operates a vital house museum that preserves the legacy of the Pabst family and their impact on the citizens, history, and culture of the Greater Milwaukee community.

In 1890, Captain Frederick Pabst, owner of the Pabst Brewing Company, hired the local Milwaukee architectural firm of George Bowman Ferry and Alfred Clas to design an opulent residence. The house was built at a cost of $250,000 (over $33 million today), and in a prominent location on of Milwaukee's most illustrious residential areas, Grand Avenue. The Pabst family resided in the house until 1908, at which point they sold it at a fraction of its cost to the Roman Catholic Archdiocese, who maintained the house primarily as the Bishop's residence until 1974. They hired the firm of Brust & Brust to analyze the site, and the firm's results determined that if the site did not receive necessary and urgent structural repair, it would fall into complete and irreversible disrepair within five years. The Archdiocese decided to sell the mansion in 1974, which was an inopportune time to put a historic house on the market. At that time, Grand Avenue was unpopular with buyers due to increasing crime rates and economic decline in the area, and the energy crisis of the early 1970s made the necessary costs associated with maintaining large structures unappealing. While City of Milwaukee officials recognized the mansion as a worthy emblem of historical Milwaukee and its identification with the brewing

Figure 1.5. National Register of Historic Places Registration Form.

NPS Form 10-900
United States Department of the Interior
National Park Service

OMB No. 1024-0018

National Register of Historic Places Registration Form

This form is for use in nominating or requesting determinations for individual properties and districts. See instructions in National Register Bulletin, *How to Complete the National Register of Historic Places Registration Form.* If any item does not apply to the property being documented, enter "N/A" for "not applicable." For functions, architectural classification, materials, and areas of significance, enter only categories and subcategories from the instructions.

1. Name of Property

Historic name: _____

Other names/site number: _____

Name of related multiple property listing: _____

(Enter "N/A" if property is not part of a multiple property listing

2. Location

Street & number: _____

City or town: _____ State: _____ County: _____

Not For Publication: ☐   Vicinity: ☐

3. State/Federal Agency Certification

As the designated authority under the National Historic Preservation Act, as amended,

I hereby certify that this ___ nomination ___ request for determination of eligibility meets the documentation standards for registering properties in the National Register of Historic Places and meets the procedural and professional requirements set forth in 36 CFR Part 60.

In my opinion, the property ___ meets ___ does not meet the National Register Criteria. I recommend that this property be considered significant at the following level(s) of significance:

___**national**   ___**statewide**   ___**local**

Applicable National Register Criteria:

___**A**   ___**B**   ___**C**   ___**D**

Signature of certifying official/Title: **Date**

State or Federal agency/bureau or Tribal Government

In my opinion, the property ___ meets ___ does not meet the National Register criteria.

Signature of commenting official: **Date**

Title :   **State or Federal agency/bureau or Tribal Government**

1

Name of Property   County and State

4. National Park Service Certification

I hereby certify that this property is:

___ entered in the National Register

___ determined eligible for the National Register

___ determined not eligible for the National Register

___ removed from the National Register

___ other (explain:) _____

Signature of the Keeper   Date of Action

5. Classification

Ownership of Property

(Check as many boxes as apply.)

Private: [ ]

Public – Local   [ ]

Public – State   [ ]

Public – Federal   [ ]

Category of Property

(Check only **one** box.)

Building(s)   [ ]

District   [ ]

Site   [ ]

Structure   [ ]

Object   [ ]

Name of Property   County and State

Number of Resources within Property
(Do not include previously listed resources in the count)

Contributing	Noncontributing	
_____	_____	buildings
_____	_____	sites
_____	_____	structures
_____	_____	objects
_____	_____	Total

Number of contributing resources previously listed in the National Register _____

6. Function or Use
Historic Functions
(Enter categories from instructions.)

_____
_____
_____
_____
_____
_____
_____

Current Functions
(Enter categories from instructions.)

_____
_____
_____
_____
_____

_____
Name of Property   County and State

7. Description

Architectural Classification
(Enter categories from instructions.)

_____
_____
_____
_____
_____
_____

Materials: (enter categories from instructions.)
Principal exterior materials of the property: _____

Narrative Description
(Describe the historic and current physical appearance and condition of the property. Describe contributing and noncontributing resources if applicable. Begin with **a summary paragraph** that briefly describes the general characteristics of the property, such as its location, type, style, method of construction, setting, size, and significant features. Indicate whether the property has historic integrity.)

Summary Paragraph

Name of Property   County and State

Narrative Description

Name of Property   County and State

8. Statement of Significance

Applicable National Register Criteria
(Mark "x" in one or more boxes for the criteria qualifying the property for National Register listing.)

☐   A. Property is associated with events that have made a significant contribution to the broad patterns of our history.

☐   B. Property is associated with the lives of persons significant in our past.

☐   C. Property embodies the distinctive characteristics of a type, period, or method of construction or represents the work of a master, or possesses high artistic values, or represents a significant and distinguishable entity whose components lack individual distinction.

☐   D. Property has yielded, or is likely to yield, information important in prehistory or history.

Criteria Considerations
(Mark "x" in all the boxes that apply.)

☐   A. Owned by a religious institution or used for religious purposes

☐   B. Removed from its original location

☐   C. A birthplace or grave

☐   D. A cemetery

☐   E. A reconstructed building, object, or structure

☐   F. A commemorative property

☐   G. Less than 50 years old or achieving significance within the past 50 years

Name of Property   County and State

Areas of Significance
(Enter categories from instructions.)

_____
_____
_____
_____
_____
_____
_____

Period of Significance

_____
_____
_____

Significant Dates

_____
_____
_____

Significant Person
(Complete only if Criterion B is marked above.)

_____
_____
_____

Cultural Affiliation

_____
_____
_____

Architect/Builder

_____
_____
_____

Name of Property   County and State

Statement of Significance Summary Paragraph (Provide a summary paragraph that includes level of significance, applicable criteria, justification for the period of significance, and any applicable criteria considerations.)

Narrative Statement of Significance (Provide at least **one** paragraph for each area of significance.)

Name of Property   County and State

9. Major Bibliographical References

Bibliography (Cite the books, articles, and other sources used in preparing this form.)

Previous documentation on file (NPS):

____ preliminary determination of individual listing (36 CFR 67) has been requested
____ previously listed in the National Register
____ previously determined eligible by the National Register
____ designated a National Historic Landmark
____ recorded by Historic American Buildings Survey #_____
____ recorded by Historic American Engineering Record # _____
____ recorded by Historic American Landscape Survey # _____

Primary location of additional data:

____ State Historic Preservation Office
____ Other State agency
____ Federal agency
____ Local government
____ University
____ Other
        Name of repository: _____

Historic Resources Survey Number (if assigned): _____

10. Geographical Data

Acreage of Property _____

Name of Property   County and State

Use either the UTM system or latitude/longitude coordinates

Latitude/Longitude Coordinates (decimal degrees)
Datum if other than WGS84:_____
(enter coordinates to 6 decimal places)
1. Latitude: Longitude:

2. Latitude: Longitude:

3. Latitude: Longitude:

4. Latitude: Longitude:

Or
UTM References
Datum (indicated on USGS map):

☐ NAD 1927   or   ☐ NAD 1983

1. Zone: Easting: Northing:

2. Zone: Easting: Northing:

3. Zone: Easting: Northing:

4. Zone: Easting :   Northing:

Verbal Boundary Description (Describe the boundaries of the property.)

Name of Property   County and State

Boundary Justification (Explain why the boundaries were selected.)

---

11. Form Prepared By

name/title: _____

organization: _____

street & number: _____

city or town: _____ state: _____ zip code:_____

e-mail_____

telephone:_____

date:_____

Additional Documentation

Submit the following items with the completed form:

• **Maps:** A **USGS map** or equivalent (7.5 or 15 minute series) indicating the property's location.

• **Sketch map** for historic districts and properties having large acreage or numerous resources. Key all photographs to this map.

• **Additional items:** (Check with the SHPO, TPO, or FPO for any additional items.)

Name of Property   County and State

Photographs

Submit clear and descriptive photographs. The size of each image must be 1600x1200 pixels (minimum), 3000x2000 preferred, at 300 ppi (pixels per inch) or larger. Key all photographs to the sketch map. Each photograph must be numbered and that number must correspond to the photograph number on the photo log. For simplicity, the name of the photographer, photo date, etc. may be listed once on the photograph log and doesn't need to be labeled on every photograph.

Photo Log

Name of Property:

City or Vicinity:

County: State:

Photographer:

Date Photographed:

Description of Photograph(s) and number, include description of view indicating direction of camera:

1 of ___ .

industry, they publicly stated that "prospective buyers of the $500,000 property would probably demolish the site," and their resignation caused a public outcry.[13]

While still legally under the ownership of the Archdiocese, advocates organized to designate the house. They successfully applied to the Milwaukee Landmarks Commission for Milwaukee Landmark status in 1974, and the house was also placed on the National Register later that year. The designations, however, could not stop the sale of the mansion, and it was purchased in December 1974 by a developer who owned a hotel on the adjacent lot and planned to raze the house to expand the parking lot.

Advocates fought back. The Milwaukee Landmarks Commission issued a public statement condemning the sale and planned demolition. The *Milwaukee Journal* and other publications decried the sale. Ultimately, the public unity worked: a new sale agreement was drafted in which the developer agreed to purchase and demolish only the carriage house on the site to allow for only a minor expansion of the hotel parking lot and did not pursue purchase of the mansion itself.

The community did not waste any time organizing management of the house as a historic site. Though the designations they had sought had not protected the house from sale, they had empowered and informed the community as to the intrinsic historical value of the mansion, and they immediately built upon that momentum. Wisconsin Heritages, Inc. was formed, and they successfully sought 501(c)(3) status to maintain the mansion as a public site. In 1978, the Captain Frederick Pabst Mansion was opened to the public. It has remained open ever since, maintaining generous public support. Current Executive Director John Eastman explains that the house is inextricably linked to its community in both history and preservation, and that it is "a house in Milwaukee for all Milwaukeeans."[14]

What can we learn?

- While designations alone cannot prevent sale or demolition of a site, they can raise public awareness and sympathy for its preservation.

- The greatest window for opportunity in terms of organization is directly following the preservation of a site, when the momentum from preservation can be harnessed for operational efforts.

* * *

Board Development

Whether you have formally worked together to seek designations, have participated in past community projects, or have simply shared the same goal of preservation, you are likely part of a contingent of community members who are like-minded in their interest to operate the site as a museum. These people will most likely form the basis of your board.

Notice that I am careful not to say that all of the people who voiced support for preservation will join your board. For some, they may view issues with a prolonged and unavoidable conflict of interest, for they might serve in elected positions that preside over the area (though these individuals can serve as strategic partners). For others, they might be faced with a matter of time investment or something else. These reasons are all okay—you should not push anyone to join the board of your burgeoning site unless he or she is fully committed. The creation of a new board requires focused attention of a group of people you want to make sure are totally engaged.

The choice is entirely yours when establishing the founding board of an organization, though I will offer a couple of recommendations. Successful boards, especially for young organizations, are usually composed of representatives from the local business community as well as those who can offer useful professional insights. Realtors, lawyers, financial managers, and, of course, museum professionals are good choices to augment your institutional knowledge base as you get started. Since you will not be able to hire staff or arrange for contracted services until you are formally incorporated, acquiring shared knowledge and skills from a participatory board is essential.

Many boards consist of a mixture of members that follow a

"give-get" system in which they either offer financial support themselves or solicit it from others. Others define their roles more broadly as a funding board, more inclined to offer donations than time, or a service board, which contributes services, professional knowledge and connections, and volunteer hours. Considering the needs of a board for new organization, I recommend prioritizing those willing to offer service. The financial needs of a site are of utmost importance, but you are dead in the water, so to speak, if you do not have a core group of board members to foster the initial stages of organizational establishment. One thing at a time, and structure comes before everything else.

I'll offer a final thought on board development in relation to the other topics covered in this chapter. The processes discussed in terms of incorporation can be lengthy, which is not to mention the time you will devote to working as a group to formulate strategic and first steps. Your incorporation will formally define your museum as a legal entity, but I encourage you to function at the standard of boards as soon as you make the decision to organize. Take minutes at meetings. Observe the rules of the quorum (majority) and vote on all decisions. Begin drafting bylaws as soon as you start meeting, and be ready to enact them once incorporation is approved. Documentation is your best friend, and a strong paper trail will not only help from a procedural standpoint but it is also the first step in creating your own history—that of the organization.

* * *

Case Study: The Louis Armstrong House Museum
Queens, New York

Mission: The mission of the Louis Armstrong House Museum is to operate the Louis Armstrong House, a National Historic Landmark and a New York City landmark, as a historic house museum; collect, arrange, preserve, catalog, and make available to the public materials relating to the life and career of Louis Armstrong; serve as a reference

source for information about Louis Armstrong; present public programs, such as concerts and lectures, that preserve and promote the
cultural legacy of Louis Armstrong.

Designed by architect Robert Johnson and built by Thomas Daly,
the house Louis and Lucille Armstrong purchased in 1943 was
a modest one in the residential neighborhood of Queens. The
Armstrongs resided together in their home until Louis's death
in 1971 and Lucille's passing in 1983, after which point the house
transferred ownership to the Louis Armstrong Educational
Foundation, which Louis founded in 1969 to promote music
education and ultimately to oversee his estate.

The house was declared a National Historic Landmark in
1975, and in 1986 it transferred ownership from the Foundation
to the New York City Department of Cultural Affairs, with an
arrangement in place for Queens College to administer the
house as a museum. Plans to formalize administration of the
house soon fell second to the task of archiving Louis Armstrong's extensive records, discovered in the house in 1986. In
1988, the house was declared a New York City landmark and in
1991, the first employee devoted to the site was hired, archivist
Michael Cogswell. Cogswell not only archived the Armstrong
collection but proved to have a knack for fundraising and
engagement and later took over stalled efforts to administer the
house as a museum. Cogswell had no background in museums,
but explained that he "bought a stack of books from AAM and
talked to every historic house museum professional I could
find."[15] His efforts proved successful, and in 1998, the house was
adapted as a museum.

A period of preservation and restoration soon followed
between 2000 and 2003, and it was incorporated in 2008. Though
the Louis Armstrong House Museum was a subsidiary of
Queens College, Cogswell thought it important to incorporate
independently of Queens College to increase funding opportunities from grant-making agencies that do not fund fiscal con-
duits (those that are stewarded) and from individuals who
preferred to deal directly with the site, not the college. The incorporation also allowed for Cogswell to form a board of directors

dedicated to the Armstrong Museum, which includes the college president and vice president. The museum also maintains an advisory board of community members and civic leaders, a vehicle by which to reverse a tenuous relationship between the college and the community.

What can we learn?

- The road to full operation as a public site can be a long one. Embrace the opportunities for growth as they come: for the Armstrong Museum, it was processing the archives first.
- Take advantages of resources such as colleagues and texts to enhance your knowledge of museum management, even with a limited background.
- Protect your assets and maintain a transparent line of communication in dealings with a steward organization.

* * *

Conclusion

In this chapter, we have discussed the necessary first steps in situating yourself as a historic site. By ensuring that you are doing everything in your power to fully document your site, its goals, key players, and your action plan, you are in a prime position to move forward by way of introducing yourself to the next and equally vital phase of action: bringing in funds.

Key Points: Checklist

We have run through a large amount of information in this chapter. Here is a brief checklist of the topics described so you can ensure you are aware of all matters that you may need to address.

- Mission Statement
- Strategic Plan
- Business Plan

- Incorporation
  - Articles of Incorporation
  - Bylaws
  - Application for Employer Identification Number (EIN)
  - Request for Tax Exemption
  - Power of Attorney and Declaration of Representative and/or Tax Information Authorization
- State Documents (check your state regulations, but you may be required to submit any of the following):
  - Name Reservation Request
  - State Charter
  - Declaration of Trust
- Memorandum of Understanding
- Historic Designations
- Develop a Working Board

Notes

1. For ease, I will provide all direction to "you" throughout this book. Without specific knowledge of how oversight, management, and work is divided among board, staff, and volunteers at your site, please note that the "you" is collective to any and all involved.

2. Mount Vernon Ladies' Association, "The Mission of the Mount Vernon Ladies' Association," George Washington's Mount Vernon, Mountvernon.org, accessed October 1, 2016, http://www.mountvernon.org/about/our-mission.

3. McFaddin-Ward House, "The McFaddin-Ward House Museum: Mission Statement," McFaddin-Ward House, accessed October 1, 2016, http://mc faddin-ward.org/about/.

4. Malibu Adamson House Foundation, "Mission Statement," Historic Adamson House and Malibu Lagoon Museum, accessed October 1, 2016, http://www.adamsonhouse.org/main.html.

5. Internal Revenue Service, "Suggested Language for Corporations and Associations (per Publication 557)," IRS.gov, accessed October 5, 2016, https://www.irs.gov/charities-non-profits/suggested-language-for-corpora tions-and-associations.

6. Ibid.

7. Ibid.

8. State of Georgia, "Name Reservation Request," sos.ga.gov, accessed October 5, 2016, http://sos.ga.gov/corporations/acrobat/applications/Form %20-%20Name%20Reservations.pdf.

9. New York State Museum, "Charter a Museum or Historical Society," nysm.nysed.gov, accessed October 10, 2016, http://www.nysm.nysed.gov/chartering/museum.

10. Association of Academic Museums and Galleries, "Best Practices," aamg-us.org, accessed October 10, 2016, https://www.aamg-us.org/wp/best-practices/.

11. National Park Service, "National Register of Historic Places Program: Nomination Forms," nps.gov, accessed October 16, 2016, https://www.nps.gov/nr/publications/forms.htm.

12. David Weible, "National Register Guide: Appendix E: National Register vs. National Historic Landmark Designations," National Trust for Historic Preservation, accessed October 17, 2016, https://savingplaces.org/stories/national-register-guide-appendix-e#.WBdm3XgXTi4.

13. John Eastberg, *The Captain Frederick Pabst Mansion: An Illustrated History* (Milwaukee, WI: Captain Frederick Pabst Mansion, 2009), 231.

14. Rebekah Beaulieu, "Accounting for the Past: Historic House Museums and the American Urban Midwest" (PhD diss., Boston University, 2017).

15. Michael Cogswell, personal communication, October 27, 2016.

2

The Welcome Mat

Understanding Contributed Income

Incorporation? Done. 501(c)(3) tax status? Confirmed. Mission statement, strategic plan, and working business plan? In the bag. All this is done, right? Good.

And if not, stop right here and complete what you have not finished. You don't want to even consider bringing in donations until you have those items completed. To not lay a proper legal foundation for your site is a disservice to both you and your constituency. You cannot properly process and acknowledge donations until you are officially incorporated and confirmed your tax-exempt status, which in turn means that your donors will not be able to write off any contributions to your organization as tax deductions. In fact, many experienced donors will ask to see your IRS determination letter before considering a donation.

Let's assume you've taken the necessary steps and now we're all on the same page about the importance of sequencing incorporation and related activities before handling contributed income. You've incorporated, perhaps you have achieved a designation, and now you're ready to graciously accept the donations people should clearly be lining up at the door (which probably needs a fresh coat of paint) to offer you! But where are they? You now need to create a strategy for engaging donors and managing contributed income. In this chapter, we will explore how to prepare for the intake and processing of donations, the different types of contributed income to solicit, and how to properly acknowledge and process such donations.

A note before you start fundraising: asking for money can be one of the most uncomfortable tasks an individual can face, be it for personal or professional reasons. Until now, your work has been mainly internal, collaborating with other like-minded individuals who share your passion for the preservation and public consumption of your site. Your to-do list has involved working to save a site and formally organize it for others, and you most likely have been ensconced in a cozy circle with other volunteers or newly minted board members who see the value of your endeavor. While the prospect of asking for support may be a daunting one—which you knew was coming—it can prove to be an intimidating hurdle for many. With that in mind, I have three tips that I hope will offer some perspective and perhaps give you a little confidence as you get started:

- Do your research. An easy place to start conceptualizing a fundraising plan and how best to engage your community is to educate yourself. There are many fantastic blogs and publications to help you explore strategies for fundraising. We will go over some basic concepts in this chapter, but there is plenty more to learn and there are countless resources to guide you. Another way to best prepare yourself is to research your local community. Whether you have been a resident for one year or ten years, you are going to experience your local, state, and regional community from the perspective of a fundraiser, perhaps for the first time. Which local organizations have reached success in fundraising at the local level? Many nonprofits publish their list of donors annually, and perhaps their board or staff would be willing to share insights. Which organizations do you regularly hear of as funding local nonprofit initiatives, and which local businesses sponsor events? Get your wheels turning about your community and the opportunities out there—as well as those organizations that receive support—because they are an essential and ongoing component of the fundraising process.

- Share your passion. As in the last chapter, I will provide some tips and information to help you learn to situate yourself in the nonprofit and preservation communities. No one, however, can take that first step except for you. Get comfortable talking and writing about your institution. Remember your mission, the history and future goals of your site, and be ready to talk about it whenever possible. You never know when a friendly conversation could evolve into donor cultivation. Your dentist may very well have gone sledding in the backyard of the house you just saved, but you may never learn that unless you make the effort to engage people and inspire them to be passionate about your site.
- Diversify your asks and don't put all your eggs in one basket. This chapter introduces you to a variety of fundraising opportunities. Some may be just right for your site, others less so. Make sure to plan for a variety of avenues by which to raise funds. For example, if a lucrative company that has offered a major annual sponsorship relocates to another town, that loss is much less painful when you have other options to bring in money.
- Have fun! Seriously. Fundraising is essentially sharing your story and inviting others to support your adventure and make it theirs as well. The difference between a genial conversation about your progress and plans and a fundraising-minded one is the addition of one question. The worst that can happen is that you do not receive a donation. This does not mean that you are a failure at fundraising, or that your project is not worthwhile. Just as you approach potential donors with an agenda, so do the people and institutions you ask have priorities, goals, and perhaps hardships to consider. Do not take it personally as a rejection—trust me, every single person who asks for money has been turned down multiple times!—but as a learning opportunity. Even those conversations that do not result in a gift often do at a later date, as your experience grows.

Fundraising Plan

At this point, you have already defined your mission and have a working strategic plan as well as a business plan. As we've discussed, these can be updated in the future, but they provide the necessary organizational and conceptual information on which to ground your fundraising plan. Another plan, you think? I have plans coming out of my ears! Fundraising can be your most strategic asset as you create the future of your site, and I highly recommend you are cognizant of all aspects of fundraising, from donor cultivation to gift processing to planning, before actively seeking funds. A fundraising plan is your opportunity to think about and document the functional plans and goals of your organization as they relate to fundraising. Such a document should outline short-term goals, those to take place within the next six to eighteen months, as well as long-term priorities, looking five, ten, or twenty years into the future. It should be aligned with your strategic plan, which can provide a valuable roadmap as you launch fundraising, but can and should provide practical direction as well.[1] Consider the following questions as you draft a fundraising plan:

- What do you want to raise money for? Many new historic sites prioritize the operational costs necessary to open the site to the public, as well as necessary repairs, maintenance, and other capital projects. This is your brainstorming session. What funds do you need to function, what do you need for special projects, and how should such initiatives be sequenced? Consider all ideas in terms of short- and long-term goals as well as their relation to your mission and strategic plan.
- How will you receive gifts? Consider this question in its most literal terms. Will you solicit gifts via campaign letters, as in common examples of membership and annual appeal campaigns? Will you accept gifts online and if so, are you prepared to pay for an online giving service to manage such gifts? Similarly, will you accept credit card donations, for which a surcharge to the organization may

be charged? It is always a good idea to make giving to your organization as easy as possible for potential donors, but you may not be able to afford the giving platforms right off the bat.

- On what date will gifts take effect? This is one of those questions that seems like a no-brainer, but the obvious answer may be different to different people. Some would prefer the date that a gift is offered, such as the date on a check, while others would say the postmarked date or the date received by the organization. This topic can be especially important for year-end gifts, or when donors are specific about processing timeframes for tax purposes. You want to create in your fundraising plan a protocol to be followed for all gift management, and the best practice (according to the Financial Accounting Standards Board) is to consider the gift effective the date it is physically transferred to the organization. This may be the date you receive a check in the mail, a community member drops off a tangible donation for your collection, or the date of a fundraiser to which people bring cash donations.
- How and when will you acknowledge donations? You will need to document the gift in a letter—we will go over this later in this chapter—which serves essentially as a receipt for the donor. Knowing that, will you send handwritten notes, perhaps from board members, in addition to the letter for tax purposes? Will you create opportunities to publicly credit donors? Many organizations include a list of donors online or in publications (or both), and special projects—such as capital restorations—may include plaques or naming opportunities.
- What is your schedule for solicitations? Planning your appeals and grant activity as well as any special campaigns is necessary to account properly for workflow and communications. Incorporate into your plan a timeline for giving activity, and plan to keep a corresponding calendar to manage related tasks. Much of your activity will be organized into campaigns, defined as concentrated and distinct periods of solicitation for a specific purpose.

- How will you track constituents and solicitations? Are you prepared to invest in donor management software, or will you consider it in the future? My advice is to start using management software as soon as you are able, and to research which system is best for your needs. Investing in top-of-the-line systems designed for extremely large organizations may prove difficult to maneuver and unnecessary (not to mention ridiculously expensive!) as you are just getting started. Work with spreadsheets for the time being, and plan to transition to management software as funds allow. You need to make sure you track contact information of donors, contact and asks, and their giving histories.
- What's the point? Consider drafting some initial boilerplate language for your organization that can serve as a resource for conversations with donors, grant applications, and printed or online materials. Such language may document the history of the site, its significance, steps necessary for its preservation, and your organizational mission and goals. Ensuring that board members, staff, and volunteers all speak a common language is integral to successful fundraising, and I recommend starting that practice as early as possible.

The execution of nuts-and-bolts procedures should adhere to a standard protocol; if your board or staff recommend updates, make sure to document them and keep the fundraising plan current. A fundraising plan will serve only internal purposes, but it creates clarity and direction for one of the key activities of your organization. You may not know all the answers to the questions in your initial organizational phase, which is absolutely fine. Fill in the blanks as your plans become concrete and your confidence and knowledge in such procedures grow. In the meantime, be sure to designate board members to helm a development (fundraising) committee who will keep an eye on your fundraising plan.

What Are Contributions?

Sounds easy, right? A contribution is a certain amount of money that someone gives you. Well, not so fast. You're essentially correct, though there are some considerations to keep in mind. According to the IRS definition, contributions are donations for which no goods or services are rendered, for which the donor receives nothing in return and is then able to document the donation as a tax deduction.[2] Let's explore some of the most common forms and avenues of contributed income.

Monetary Gifts

The most common form of contributed income is cash gifts, which can be divided into two major funding streams: individual giving, also known as donations from people; and structured giving, which is offered by foundations, corporations, and government entities, and is usually awarded via a formal application process.

Individual Giving

For most historic sites, individual giving will be the initial and dominant activity. Don't forget your fundraising plan; create a calendar for solicitations from individuals rather than simply assuming you will find yourself in contact with community members. As you are in your earliest stages, you may elect to organize a "Friends group," which consists of core constituents with a strong interest in your site's success. If you are fortunate enough to have individuals who are interested in supporting your organization from the start and are looking for a way to define them beyond board service (which may not interest them), a Friends group is a fantastic way to honor those who provide initial and sustained support. This should be separate from your board, and may form the basis for your membership, which is the first logical campaign to organize.

Campaigns

As previously explained, a campaign is any solicitation activity for a specific purpose, and usually over a specific period. Consider beginning with a membership campaign, the most common campaign for nonprofit organizations of any type or scale. Membership campaigns can be the easiest way to build your constituency and create a regular—usually annual—solicitation of support. How to get started? Simple: build a mailing list. Publicly available information, such as tax rolls, can provide the basis for such a list; gathering recommendations of additions from board members, and researching members of and donor lists to similar organizations may be more time intensive but quite useful as well.

Once you have the membership list in progress, craft a document by which to promote membership offerings. In terms of creating your membership form, again look to similar organizations for comparison (What are their giving levels? Do they offer discounts or special benefits for higher giving levels?), also considering your unique offerings. Plan to disseminate this form by mail and perhaps email at least once a year. This will be your campaign and it will create a giving cycle. Don't restrict yourself to only a certain time frame for giving, however, and make sure to keep your form available onsite and online for easy access to those who elect to become members at any time of year.

The other major campaign initiative is the annual appeal, which is exactly what it sounds like: the annual appeal for organizational support. Some organizations roll their membership and appeal asks into a single campaign, often based on the response of their specific community. I recommend at least starting with an institutional giving year that includes a membership ask (perhaps midway through the fiscal year) as well as an annual appeal (at the end of the fiscal year). The timing of such asks is up to you, though many organizations find success with fundraising appeals that take place at the end of the year, when many individuals plan to handle their donations. Conversely, specific campaigns and associated fundraising events often take place in the fall and spring seasons, which provides some breathing room between asks. Annual appeals typically provide general support operations and programming, though other organizations prioritize special projects. Whatever your needs may be, draft a letter to explain the year's achievements and goals for the coming year, and the role such support will offer. Include in your correspondence (and online) a card or form for completion by the donor regarding their giving amount and preferred listing for a credit line, which may be their names, a business, in honor of someone else or to incorporate acknowledgment of a matching gift, or even anonymous. Make sure to credit donors wherever possible and use his or her preferred credit, noting such preferences in your donor files.

Unrestricted vs. Restricted Donations

With all monetary gifts, an organization must recognize which contributions are restricted versus those that are unrestricted. While you should plan for general annual campaigns, also consider that the funds raised for special projects will have to be documented accordingly, and will likely have to be managed outside of your operating funds as restricted funds. Unrestricted donations can be used for any needs of the organization, from heating costs to refreshments for events to staff salaries. Ideally, you want a high number of unrestricted donations, as these funds can be used at your discretion. Restricted funds are no less valuable, though are designated for a specific use. A donor may offer support for educational initiatives, or funds may be raised for a capital project, such as a room restoration. These contributions must be used for the purpose stated, and such restrictions should be documented for internal purposes and in communication with the donor. You will not have a problem if you wish to utilize unrestricted funds for a certain purpose, but you cannot use restricted funds for anything other than the defined purpose. We will talk more about financial management in chapter 4, but here I will simply recommend that you plan to code donations for easy reference and to ensure you are processing restricted contributions according to the agreed-upon conditions and uses.

Endowment

In addition to fundraising for your operating costs via regular annual campaigns, and fundraising for special projects by way of capital campaigns, at some point you will want to build an endowment. Essential to the stability of any nonprofit organization is a healthy endowment, which is a fund of invested capital from which funds are regular distributed (usually less than the income earned). At some point. you will want to build at least one endowment from which an annual distribution can be paid out for use. Endowments should be established with defined terms of use, such as the projected use for operations, acquisitions, or restoration projects.[3] A sample of endowment terms is found in figure 2.1, and includes certain components that should be a part of any endowment terms, no matter size of gift or use:

- Date
- Name of Donor
- Title of Fund
- Summary of Terms: gift restrictions (uses), notes regarding financial management of the fund including principal and distribution, and if the donor allows additional gifts to be added to the fund
- Board Action: usually the date on which the board accepted the terms of the proposed endowment and the date/description of any term updates. (Note that terms are legally binding and not usually subject to change, so updates should be rare or nonexistent.)

Many small organizations have one endowment, while others have several endowments dedicated to a variety of activities. A note to consider is that while endowments can be valuable, you will want to draft a spending policy to ensure a structure of endowment use and to keep the endowment itself growing at a rate that exceed inflation over the long term. Be sure to embark on creating an endowment only when you can commit to its proper management. Endowments can be the destination for

Figure 2.1. Sample Endowment Terms.

Historic House Museum
Anywhere, USA
Phone: 555-555   Email: xxxx@xxxx.org

Sample Endowment Terms

Date: January 1, 2016

Name of Fund: The John L. Smith Acquisition Fund

Established By: John L. Smith, founding board member of State Historical Society

Board Actions: Accepted by vote, March 15, 2016

Description:

"This Fund is to be used to provide support for the acquisitions program of the State Historical Society. The Fund is open to gifts and contributions from any source.

The income and potential realized gains of said Fund may be expended for the purposes of the The John L. Smith Acquisition Fund provided, specifically to fund the acquisition of objects related to the history and culture of State. Amounts which may be added to said Fund by gift or bequest are to be administered in the same manner."

(From letter of agreement signed by John L. Smith dated January 1, 2016)

Comments: see signed letter attached for documentation of agreement.

---

any contribution of cash or stock, but are most often grown via planned giving.

* * *

Case Study: The Woodlawn Museum, Gardens & Park
Ellsworth, Maine[4]

Mission: Under the governance of the Hancock County Trustees of Public Reservation, Woodlawn offers the people of Hancock County

and beyond opportunities for recreation and education on a preserved historic estate, and provides connections to the region's cultural heritage through programs that arouse curiosity and entertain,
and the preservation of historic facilities.[5]

In 1901, a group of citizens in Ellsworth, Maine, created the Hancock County Trustees of Public Reservations to preserve land
they were concerned was increasingly damaged by private use
and the lumber trade. The Trustees preserved thousands of acres
on Mount Desert Island, which they donated to the federal government and now comprises Acadia National Park. The group
was primarily dedicated to land conservation, until 1929, when
resident George Nixon Black Jr. bequeathed his estate, Woodlawn, to the organization. An endowment accompanied the gift
to provide for regular maintenance of the 1827 house as well as
the salary of a caretaker.

The Hancock County Trustees of Reservations remained a
volunteer-run organization until 2000, with only a seasonal caretaker and paid docents on the payroll. A volunteer committee
was responsible for the oversight of Woodlawn, limited to maintenance but with little programming offered and no focus on
operation as a public site. With an aim to professionalize the
site, the group initiated a strategic planning process and led a
campaign to raise funds for an executive director. Joshua Torrance arrived in 2000 and has been the executive director of the
Woodlawn Museum, Gardens and Park ever since. Interpreted
spaces include the 1827 house, an 1857 barn that has undergone
remodeling in 1900 and again in 1948, and a sleigh barn, which
was restored in 2008 and turned into a program space. Woodlawn also maintains a permanent collection of original furnishings as they belonged to the Black family between 1802 and
1928, decorative arts, ephemera, and archives that relate to the
Black family and to the local lumber trade.

When Torrance arrived, he was fortunate to have a positive,
optimistic, and committed board.[6] He was also fortunate to
enter an organization with an endowment in place, though he
immediately recognized the need for a funding structure. He
realized that the endowment would provide essential support

and stability to the organization, but the terms and fund balance were such that he would have to initiate new forms of fundraising.

Without much money and with virtually no staff, Torrance moved quickly. He first set up a membership program, the contacts for which he culled from tax rolls. Torrance grew the membership to 250 members, which was a priority for his first ten years. Next, he set up an annual appeal campaign. Torrance timed his appeal to take place at the end of the fiscal year and encouraged donors to fund the following year's operating budget. Whenever possible, he would and does entice contributions with a challenge grant, in which a potential gift is offered but must be matched by other contributions.

Once Woodlawn was stable and had a system that supported its operating needs, Torrance launched Woodlawn's first capital campaign to fund preservation efforts. The capital campaign goal was $1.1 million, and over two years Woodlawn received that $1.1 million from foundations, individuals, and the successful match to a challenge grant. Torrance recognized that he needed to grow the endowment of Woodlawn for long-term self-sustenance, and included endowment support in the campaign goal. Woodlawn has been in its second capital campaign with a goal of $8.2 million, 50 percent of which has been raised. Torrance explains that he considers fundraising a long arc that requires investment, but that slow growth has the benefit of sustained donor engagement.

What can we learn?

- Upon his arrival, Torrance defined the primary asset of the organization (the site) and the goal (its care and upkeep). Many historic sites and specifically historic house museums are similarly prioritized—consider this when drafting your fundraising plan.
- Once the primary asset and fundraising priority was established, the constituents were immediately engaged via membership and appeal campaigns, and maintained connection via capital campaigns. Think about how to

structure your fundraising goals for long-term donor engagement.

* * *

Planned Giving

Perhaps a donor wishes to make a major gift during their lifetime or at death. In such situations, a nonprofit may deal with the donor directly, or with a representative such as the executor of a will or a lawyer. As a component of many individuals' financial or estate planning, planned giving should be handled on a case-by-case basis and according to donors' wishes. That said, let's look at some of the most common forms of planned giving.

Bequest

When most people think of planned giving, they think of giving at the time of a donor's death, and they are usually thinking of a bequest. Bequests are transfers of wealth made at the time of death. Such gifts may have been planned, or an organization may simply receive word on behalf of the donor's estate that it has been named a beneficiary. Such gifts may be cash gifts, including gifts of stock, tangible donations, virtually anything the donor has decided to leave to the site. (To ensure that such gifts will be welcome additions and related to the mission-based activities of your site, I recommend advertising that you accept planned gifts including bequests, and would be willing to work with donors.)

Trust

A trust is akin to a will, but in a separate document that is not subject to probate. The contents of a trust can take many forms, but it is structured in one of two forms: a trust agreement or a declaration of trust. Popular with wealthy clients to minimize estate tax, a trust is a way to formalize current or future giving activity.

The building of an organizational endowment and the solicitation of planned giving relationships can often go overlooked in small nonprofits, as they require a certain amount of financial and time investment to ensure the funds are coordinated and managed properly. They are, however, invaluable cornerstones of a strong fundraising program. Do not overlook such a worthwhile fundraising avenue, especially considering that many historic sites often benefit from relationships with older donors.

Noncash Donations

While cash is essential to the function of a site, so are nonmonetary gifts, such as in-kind and tangible donations. Let's look at these two ways people can support your site beyond gifts of money.

In-Kind Gifts

Another potential form of support from local businesses is that of in-kind donations. In-kind donations are not monetary but are gifts of time, products, and services. A painter may not provide a cash gift but may offer to paint the front façade for free or for a reduced rate and public acknowledgment for donated services. In-kind gifts can also serve to match a grant award if need be. One tricky thing to keep in mind, however, is that the IRS rules are explicit regarding the deduction of in-kind gifts: no deduction is available for time or services donated, and only the direct cost of materials can be deducted. That painter, for instance, can deduct the cost of materials but not the hours donated to painting the façade. Unlike gifts of monetary value, your acknowledgment for in-kind gifts should not state the dollar value of the donation but rather the general value of the service offered. See figure 2.2 for an example of an in-kind gift acknowledgment letter.

Figure 2.2.   In-kind Gift Acknowledgment.

Historic House Museum
Anywhere, USA
Phone: 555-555   Email: xxxx@xxxx.org

In-Kind Gift Acknowledgement Letter

Date

Donor Name

Address

Dear Donor,

On behalf of <u>organization name</u>, I would like to thank you for your generous donation of <u>description of gift</u> made on <u>date of donation</u>. The work of <u>organization name</u> is made possible through the support of friends like you.

(If credit line will be made public, document here.)

While IRS regulations do not allow a declaration of value of your donation in this acknowledgement, we can offer that were it not for your generosity, we likely would have spent $(dollar amount) for such services. Your in-kind contribution allows us to devote those funds to directly support our programs and services.

Thank you once again.

Sincerely,

<u>Handwritten Signature</u>

<u>Typed Name and Title</u>

<u>Organization Name</u>
<u>Tax Exempt Number</u>

Tangible Gifts

Tangible gifts are gifts of material goods, and can range from office supplies, such as a chair or desk, to objects for a permanent collection. Most nonprofit organizations benefit from the contribution of supplies for the office or goods that aid in operations. If you choose to maintain a collection for display and interpretation, you may also seek tangible donations to build a collection, or that others will approach you with a potential object for the collection.

While many other sources delve more deeply into collections management, I will make a couple of basic recommendations from a management and financial perspective. First, make sure that you have both collections and collections management plans in place. These plans detail what you collect and how you manage the collection, and should include language related to gift acceptance processes, accessions, and deaccessions. Not only is this considered best process according to the IRS and the American Alliance of Museums (AAM) (which offers multiple resources on devising such plans), the creating of collections and collections management plans helps you to determine which objects fall into your purview to accept and which do not comply with your mission. Second, do not accept anything you cannot adequately care for, whether in terms of storage needs, conservation, display, or financial investment. When you accept a gift and accession it into the collection you are agreeing to provide adequate care for the object. Historic house museums often become repositories for discarded old items; if your site cannot care for the object, or if it is not aligned with the interpretation of the site, or if you simply do not wish to accept it, you should not accept it.

The tangible donation form follows the same acknowledgment procedure, whether for office supplies or gifts of art. It is the responsibility of the donor to provide a value of the donation to the IRS for their deduction, but they have no obligation to provide a value to the recipient of the gift. You may need to seek that information elsewhere. For basic supplies such as computers, valuations are standard and can be found in IRS literature as well as in the documentation of organizations (such as Goodwill or the Salvation Army) that regularly receive such items. For historical and art objects, the donor should seek a formal appraisal from an appraiser. Note that you should not estimate the value for an object donated to your collection; an informed third party or published reference should determine the insurance and market values. Keep a list of licensed appraisers on hand to share with donors when necessary. I would recommend including a copy of the appraisal in your financial and object records. I also recommend drafting a deed of gift document for objects to be accessioned into the permanent collection in addition to the acknowledgment letter. This details the terms of care, any restrictions or precautions regarding installation and display, and serves as a formal record of the gift for the object records as well as your financial records. You can also use this form to clarify your deaccessioning policy for the donor, which prompts the conversation with the donor about the institutional obligation to retain the object gifted. Some donors will have no preference about potential deaccessioning of the object, while others will care a great deal. Documentation of the donor's wishes regarding deaccessioning is always useful for operational purposes down the road. Figure 2.3 provides an example of a tangible donation gift acknowledgment letter.

Securities Gifts

Many individuals will elect not to give outright cash gifts, but will instead offer to transfer a gift of appreciated stock or mutual funds to the organization. These gifts are common for donors that wish to avoid capital gains, increase their deductions, or simply maximize their contribution to your organization. These are a valuable form of noncash contributions that are easier to manage than may appear at first glance. I qualify the stock as appreciated because, to make a gift of stock, the stock must have been in the possession of the donor for at least one year, and the stock must have increased in value. The value of securities gifts is determined one of two ways. If it is a gift of stock that is publicly traded, the value is determined as its average market price on the date the gift was received. If the gift is mutual funds

Figure 2.3. Tangible Donation Gift Acknowledgment.

Historic House Museum
Anywhere, USA

Phone: 555-555   Email: xxxx@xxxx.org

Sample Tangible Donation Acknowledgement Letter

Date

Donor Name

Address

Dear Donor,

On behalf of <u>organization name</u>, I would like to thank you for your generous donation of <u>description of gift</u> made on <u>date of donation</u>. The work of <u>organization name</u> is made possible through the support of friends like you.

(If credit line will be made public, document here.)

This letter serves as your receipt, and we encourage you to please keep it for your records.

Thank you once again.

Sincerely,

Handwritten Signature

Typed Name and Title

<u>Description of Donated Property:</u>

Donor is responsible for determining fair market value for the purposes of tax deduction.

<u>Organization Name</u>
<u>Tax Exempt Number</u>

---

or stock that is not publicly traded, its value is equal to the original cost.

Structured Giving

In addition to individual giving, structured giving by organizations and government entities is another major avenue of fundraising. Many corporations, foundations, and government agencies have regular giving programs, and these can provide a useful investment of time, for the gifts can be substantially larger than those raised through individual giving.

Applying for Grants

To get started with a successful grants program, commit time to research. What calls for applications are available at local, regional, and national levels? What foundations and corporations support preservation, historic sites, and the cultural sector in general? Where have organizations similar to your own realized success? What strategic activities do you wish to fund? Visit websites of organizations that offer grants and review funding parameters. You may even take notes on the credited funders of sites similar to your own, which can usually be found in publications such as newsletters or onsite.

As you accumulate information, keep a list of funding organizations and opportunities, deadlines, and grant guidelines. You will also want to detail potential opportunities in a calendar, as discussed in the section on the fundraising plan. It may be easiest to start local, where your site may be known, and because local funding agencies tend to have more simple applications, often only a letter and perhaps a budget. Keep in mind that agencies rarely fund general operations, so think about ways to present your activities that is attractive to funders: instead of asking for operating support, you will have better luck funding a lecture program, a publication, or a capital project. We will talk more about budgets in chapter 4 and how to present such information from a financial perspective. For now, consider how to set strategic priorities that will appeal to program officers at grant-making agencies.

Once you have selected opportunities to pursue, make contact. Usually, funding organizations have websites on which they list contact information for program officers. I recommend sending an email to briefly introduce your site, the project for which you plan to seek funding, and ask to set up an informational phone meeting. A common misconception about structured giving is that your relationship with agencies is faceless and nameless. You can and should, however, build contact with program officers whenever possible (some agencies make it clear they do not welcome phone calls or emails—be sure to always follow the rules as listed). If you can connect via phone, this is a fantastic opportunity to provide background on your site and the details of your potential application. Often program officers appreciate the chance to learn about your organization before reviewing an application. They may offer advice, highlight some of the topics you will want to be sure to address in your application, and provide insight into ways you can strengthen your application. This is your time to ask questions, and it is also an apt moment for the officer to tell you if your application is a good fit for their agency or the specific funding cycle. They may be prioritizing digital initiatives in a year you are undergoing a capital campaign, or they may fund community engagement when you are interested in building an archive. Don't view this as a deterrent but as extremely useful feedback that ensures you do not invest time on an application that you know will not be funded. Furthermore, officers appreciate being able to tell you if there is not an alignment between your project and the grant cycle, because it also saves them the time of reviewing the application.

If you receive the green light to move forward from a program officer—or do not have the ability to connect with an officer but feel your project application will realize success—you then draft your application. At the very least, an application will consist of a letter or short narrative, as well as a budget that contextualizes your ask amount. While narratives vary in length according to grant guidelines, a strong narrative includes the following:

- Mission of your organization and the ways in which the site benefits the community.
- Overview of the project and why it is important.
- Who the project will serve and which audiences it will positively impact.
- General timeline for completion and how you will measure success.

Budgets will be detailed in chapter 4, but most applications require at least a simple outline of expenses.

A couple of notes to consider when embarking on grant applications. Grants can be quite time intensive, so plan to invest your time wisely on a few well-done applications rather than a high number of applications that cast too wide a net. That said, the process moves more quickly if you create language that can be utilized for applications to multiple organizations, such as organizational background. You will find that project budgets and descriptions can often be reused with minor edits as required in the grant guidelines. Also, this is another case where it benefits you to know your community. You may be in a rural area, for instance, where there are no local foundations or corporations from which to seek funding. Do not be deterred, if that is the case: regional and national funding opportunities are available for historic sites, and program officers will consider geographical limitations regarding funding.

You want to follow the application guidelines that are provided to the best of your ability. Answer any questions asked clearly and completely and provide documentation when asked. Do not include any narrative information or supplemental documents that are not of direct relevance to your application and within the format offered. And it may seem clever, but funding organizations can tell if you have narrowed margins or decreased the font size so that you can include more text. Follow the rules to avoid unnecessarily disgruntling the program officers reviewing your application.

Corporate Sponsorships

Grants are not the only way to engage with businesses or corporations, and sponsorships are another great way to invite support. Usually coordinated around a stand-alone event or a series of programs, sponsorships are contributions made in exchange for public promotion. Sponsorships serve as an effective opportunity for small local businesses as well as large corporations. You can build a contact list for businesses by researching membership of your local rotary chapter or chamber of commerce as well as researching sponsors of organizations similar to your own.

As you create a list of potential sponsors, also consider what initiatives you propose for sponsorship support. Usually promotion is key in successful sponsorship agreements, and marketing and brand-building are just as important as philanthropic goals for sponsors. Knowing this, consider events and programs first. A sponsor may contribute to a special event, or they could sponsor multiple events, such as a lecture series. Approach businesses with a sponsorship plan that delineates giving levels and sponsor benefits (see figure 2.4 for an example). Consider making personal contact with potential sponsors in person or by phone, and follow up with your sponsorship plan as well as event details and background on your site. Benefits may include guest passes or free attendance at events, sponsor signage, verbal acknowledgment during events, or links to sponsor businesses on your website. Building relationships with sponsors can be an extremely productive and lucrative activity from which both parties benefit.

Gift Acknowledgments

All gifts, no matter how received and whether monetary, tangible, or in-kind, necessitate acknowledgment. Provided thus far in chapter 2 are acknowledgments of restricted gifts (an endowment), in-kind gifts, and tangible gifts. A general acknowledgment sample is offered in figure 2.5. Though technically only required by the IRS for gifts valued at $250 and above, I recommend acknowledging all gifts you receive for clear documentation of the transaction for the donor and internal records. (An

Figure 2.4.   Corporate Sponsorship example.

Historic House Museum
Anywhere, USA
Phone: 555-555   Email: xxxx@xxxx.org

Historic House Tour

Sponsorship Levels

$1,000 SUPPORTING SPONSOR

• 6 complimentary tickets to the House event

• Your name/company listed on all House Tour advertisements, marketing materials & brochure

• Acknowledgment in all media releases and signage at the event

• Logo display on House website

• Your name or company logo w/link to your website on the THPT website through December 31, 2014

$500 CONTRIBUTING SPONSOR

• 4 complimentary tickets to the House event

• Your name/company listed on all House advertisements, marketing materials & brochure

• Acknowledgment in all media releases and signage at the event

• Logo display on House website

$250 PATRON SPONSOR

• 2 complimentary tickets to the House event

• Your name/company and logo listed on all House advertisements, marketing materials & brochure

• Acknowledgment in all media releases and signage at the event
----
If you wish to have your logo or business card included in event brochure, please email a jpeg to xxxxx@xxxxx.org by DATE. Any questions, please call (xxx) xxx-xxxx.

NAME OF SPONSOR (How you wish to be listed):
ADDRESS:

CONTACT NAME:	DAY PHONE: ( )	EMAIL:	
PLEASE CIRCLE HOUSE TOUR SPONSOR AMOUNT:		$250 $500	$1,000
SPONSOR NAME:	TITLE:	SIGNATURE:	DATE:

MAIL CHECK AND APPLICATION TO:

exception to this rule is donation boxes. The anonymity of the cash contributions is nearly impossible to track and is usually given without expectation of acknowledgment.)

Please note that the acknowledgment is different from a credit. For financial purposes, your acknowledgment is the receipt for the transaction and acts as record for possible tax deductions. A credit is the public recognition of a donor's gift and can be listed in wall labels, publications, or plaques. All donations should require an acknowledgment, but only some necessitate a credit line. Sizable individual or family contributions, gifts from corporations and foundations, and others will warrant public promotion at your discretion.

Since your acknowledgment is a formal document, it should incorporate certain elements. On any gift acknowledgment, be sure to include the following:

- Organizational letterhead at top.
- Tax Identification Number (EIN).
- Amount of gift, the date on which gift was received, and the key language that "no goods or services were received in exchange for payment," since this is what the IRS must confirm for tax deduction purposes. Take the opportunity to comment on the value of the donor and the integral role such donations play in the success of your site.
- Though not required, a personal touch is always welcome. A handwritten signature from a board member or a brief note makes the correspondence personal, friendly, and most importantly, donor-centric.

Gift Reporting

All fundraising is cyclical. You begin with research, then move into donor contact and cultivation, formally ask for funding, execute initiatives utilizing funding, and then report back to the funder, known as stewardship. This is an extremely important step and must not be overlooked, for it concludes one project and, one hopes, lays the groundwork for the next. While the

Figure 2.5.   General Donation Acknowledgment.

Historic House Museum
Anywhere, USA

Phone: 555-555   Email: xxxx@xxxx.org

SAMPLE DONOR ACKNOWLEDGEMENT LETTER

Date

Donor Name

Address

Dear Donor,

On behalf of <u>organization name</u>, I would like to thank you for your generous donation of $ <u>amount</u> made on <u>date of donation</u>. The work of <u>organization name</u> is made possible through the support of friends like you.

(If credit line will be made public, document here.)

Your donation is tax deductible to the fullest extent allowed by the law. No goods or services were provided in return for your donation. This letter serves as your receipt, and we encourage you to please keep it for your records.
Thank you once again.

Sincerely,

<u>Handwritten Signature</u>

<u>Typed Name and Title</u>

<u>Organization Name</u>
<u>Tax Exempt Number</u>

responsibilities for reporting to individual donors and to structured funding opportunities is a bit different, the goal is the same: document how the donation was used, the success of the project, and the exciting plans for the future, which you hope to discuss with the donor (all, of course, while profusely thanking the donor for the support they offered). Note that these steps of relationship-building should be taken in addition to your gift acknowledgments, which serve as documentation of the transaction.

Reporting to Individual Donors

For individuals, your reporting will usually be quite general. For those that gave to membership or annual campaigns (or both), the gift can be acknowledged with the formal letter and an update on the organization, wrapped into general correspondence, which is most likely the next year's ask. Consider creating a threshold for those higher-level gifts—perhaps about $250 or $500—that warrant a more personalized response. Or, perhaps you wish to recognize those that gave to a specific campaign and to keep them informed, or you wish to update those that set up longer-term giving over time. Stewardship for donors usually consists of a letter that reports on activities since the gift was received and how it has been a service to the organization. The purpose of individual donor stewardship, just like cultivation, is to make the individual feel like a participant. To not send a stewardship letter may lead to a donor wondering where their gift went, which could leave them feeling uninformed and unlikely to give again. You can send stewardship donors to letters upon project completion or annually: just make sure to create a habit of reporting to your donors regarding their contributions. Initiating such correspondence sets a positive tone for future solicitations and strengthens relationships with donors.

Grant Stewardship

For structured giving, the reporting is a bit different. Many grant-making agencies are quite clear in their reporting expectations. They may inform you when a stewardship report is to be submitted, either by a certain date or at the conclusion of the funded project. The funding program may request a narrative report in the form of a letter, a financial report detailing how funds were spent, or the report may be structured into responses to questions related to attendance, project execution, or an evaluation of how goals were met. If you receive a grant and the award letter does not explicate guidelines for reporting, simply send an email to the program or your program officer to ask. Whatever direction they provide, be prepared to describe the activities made possible by the gift and how you hope to approach them in the future. Much like your reporting to individuals, grant stewardship is a chance to formally close the circle on one gift and prepare you and the grant-making agency for a future ask.

*   *   *

Case Study: The Gamble House
Pasadena, California

> Mission: The Gamble House in Pasadena, California, is an outstanding example of American Arts and Crafts style architecture. The house and furnishings were designed by architects Charles and Henry Greene in 1908 for David and Mary Gamble of the Procter & Gamble Company. The house, designated a National Historic Landmark in 1978, is owned by the City of Pasadena and operated by the University of Southern California.[7]

The Gamble House was originally constructed in 1908, designed by the firm of Greene and Greene as a winter residence for David and Mary Gamble. The house has remained popular as a well-known example of Arts and Crafts architecture with its integration into the landscape, Japanese-inspired aesthetic, and embrace of natural materials. (If you're not into Arts and Crafts architecture, you may at least know the Gamble House as Dr. Emmett Brown's house in *Back to the Future*.)

The house was a private residence and stayed in the Gamble family until 1966, when Cecil and Louise Gamble gifted the house to the University of Southern California (USC) School of

Architecture. Because USC is a private university chartered by the State of California, the City of Pasadena owns the house, which is maintained and operated by the School of Architecture. The house was designated a National Historic Landmark in 1978 and remains under USC stewardship. While the house is stewarded by a large university with which it maintains a strong relationship, director Edward Bosley still prioritizes public engagement and fundraising.

The programs and activities of the Gamble House are diverse, and so is its fundraising plan. There is a dedicated membership group, composed of individual and corporate members focused on general support of the house, specifically related to restoration and preservation. The membership is divided into tiers for individuals as well as business members from small businesses ($1,000) to corporate members ($5,000). In addition to funding capital needs, the fund also supports the Scholar-in-Residence program, through which two fifth-year architecture students reside in the house each year. The program melds public investment in education, care of the property, and the USC steward, an effective integration of stakeholders and priorities. The site also maintains an active annual campaign to fund specific projects; in 2015, $100,000 was sought to apply preservative to the exterior.

The house effectively leverages its public position as a well-known site to raise funds and engage with the community. Speakers visit schools and organizations on behalf of the Gamble House and often in advance of tours to share the history of the site, and do so in exchange for a donation. The site also maintains a junior docent program, which works with local schools to educate interested students about the house and certify them as docents. This engages the students as well as their parents, who are apt to give in exchange for such an educational opportunity.

In 2003 and 2004, Bosley led a capital campaign in the amount of $3.5 million to fund exterior restoration of the Gamble House. Funds were spent as they were raised, and the website and newsletter of the site offered monthly updates that included plans and photographs of their progress at every stage of the project. Their progress reports credited recent donors to the project, and included smaller goals to be met each month on the way to project completion. Today, the restoration campaign webpage is still live and had such a positive impact that it is a standard by which other Gamble House campaigns are structured. The webpage serves as a reminder of successful project management and funding to potential donors, and also lays the groundwork for current capital projects, such as an ongoing landscaping initiative.

What can we learn?

- Make no assumption that because a site is stewarded by a parent organization that dedicated fundraising is unnecessary. All sites, regardless of size and at all stages of existence, must fundraise in order to support operational needs and special projects.
- Keep your constituency apprised of project progress, especially with capital projects. Make it easy for them to give and stay engaged with updates and goals at various levels.

* * *

Conclusion

Contributed income is vital to your success as a 501(c)(3) organization. This chapter has offered explanation of the various ways to coordinate your fundraising plan, outreach to potential funders, and document donations and properly acknowledge donors. Now that you have a foundation for understanding how to raise money, let's discuss the other form of revenue generation: earning money.

Key Points: Checklist

In this chapter, we have introduced several concepts and procedures related to contributed income. The following includes a checklist of topics to address and items to draft. Unlike the first chapter, you may not need to follow all recommendations; remember to know your community and your constituency.

- Background Preparation
  - Mission Statement
  - Strategic Plan
  - Business Plan
- Fundraising Plan
  - Development Committee
- Monetary Contributions
  - Individual Giving
    - Membership Form and Acknowledgment
    - Annual Appeal Form
    - Endowment Terms
  - Planned Giving
- Noncash Donations
  - In-Kind Gifts
  - Tangible Gifts
  - Securities Gifts
- Structured Giving
  - Grants Calendar
  - Grants Planning
  - Corporate Sponsorships
- Gift Acknowledgments
- Gift Reporting

Notes

1. See Juilee Decker, "Introduction," in *Fundraising and Strategic Planning: Innovative Approaches for Museums* (Lanham, MD: Rowman & Littlefield, 2015).

2. To play devil's advocate, let's say that a donor does receive *something* in return. All of us have seen PBS pledge drives that tell us that you get a DVD or a tote bag or a snazzy umbrella (or some other item not nearly worth the price of the giving level) with your $150 gift. Why is that, and how does the system work? This falls under what is known as a "quid-pro quo" contribution, in which the IRS states that the tax-deductible amount is "limited to the excess of any money (and the value of any property other than money) contributed by the donor over the fair market value of goods or services provided by the charity." That means that the donation, for tax purposes, is the amount after the value of the gift is deducted, and the donor must be issued a statement of disclosure (which can be included in the acknowledgment) of the difference between the donation offered and that which can be considered tax-deductible. The IRS does make allowances for so-called token items, usually

gifts that bear the logo of the institution and have a value under $25. If you're confused, you are not alone, and the IRS has issued multiple reports that document their policies regarding such goods. My recommendation is to simply avoid gifts offered in exchange for donations. Such objects can be sold for earned revenue, and can be offered in special cases to donors as long as the cost of which is documented in the institutional accounts.

3. See Anita Lichtblau, "Endowments and Restricted Gifts: Accessible or 'Hands Off'?" in *The Legal Guide for Museum Professionals*, ed. Julia Courtney (Lanham, MD: Rowman & Littlefield, 2015).

4. Interview with Joshua Torrance, Executive Director.

5. https://woodlawnmuseum.com/about-2/.

6. Joshua Torrance, personal communication, November 21, 2016.

7. https://gamblehouse.org/mission-statement/.

3

Brick by Brick

Earned Revenue Opportunities

Once you have formally organized, you will not only be in a position to raise money but also to earn money. The balance between contributed, earned income, and income from funds and investments (such as your endowment distribution) is a valuable one, and the activities should indeed coexist. While fostering donor relations and creating opportunities for giving is imperative, earned revenue streams are also necessary. For any nonprofit business, whether a theater company, art museum, or historical society, a diversification of funding streams—between contributions and earnings, and within those two categories—should be your goal. Thinking about contributed and earned income in tandem is important for reasons of stability. Since contributions can have consequences based on economic shifts and other variables, it is best to plan for income that is structured beyond a system of donations. Such an arrangement ensures that you are not overly reliant on any one form of income, which provides for better short- and long-term financial solidity.

You also want to think about how to create and systematize a variety of income streams within both categories of contributed and earned income. In the last chapter, we talked about having regular appeal and membership campaigns, organizing grant and corporate giving opportunities, and special project campaigns, among other things. Together, these provide an array of giving options for potential donors. The same should be the case for your earned revenue offerings. Are you wondering what that means in practice? Consider this example: you have a historic house museum that is a desirable and successful venue for private rentals. You are confident in budget projections based on 50 percent of your income from contributions and the other 50 percent entirely of earnings from rentals. In the middle of the summer, your busiest season for private events and your most important time of year for earned revenue from rental activity, a major rainstorm causes your paved front entrance to buckle, which requires you to close your doors to clients while your driveway is regraded and repaved. Not only does this cost you the income you counted on, you now have a capital project to fund—and potentially disgruntled clients in whom to invest valuable staff time.

Unfortunately, unforeseen capital projects are no surprise to historic site professionals. But you are only making yourself more vulnerable to long-term budget implications when such situations arise if you are too dependent on one avenue of earned revenue to balance a budget. The hypothetical situation I just outlined would not be nearly as dire if the forecasted earned income included other income streams such as online shop sales or archival research fees, less based on the appearance and general accessibility of your site. In this chapter, we will define earned income, discuss some of the most common forms that you can implement at your museum, and how most strategically to launch such programs.

Earned Revenue and How to Prepare

Earned income is the revenue generated from the sale of goods or services rendered. The difference between earned and contributed incomes is quite simple: contributions are money generated for which nothing is received in return, and earnings are generated from offering something for sale.

Strategic Considerations

In the first two chapters, we discussed the importance of under-standing your community, whether in terms of the establish-ment and formal organization of your site, or in building of membership tiers and giving levels. Such an exercise is no less valuable for earned income, and just as you need to create a climate of engagement for people to *give* money, so do you need to do so for people to *spend* money. There are a couple of simple ways you can think about your community and the role you can serve that can set the foundation for successful earned giving options.

Market Evaluations

Just as you aim to generally situate yourself within your com-munity as a new organization and one seeking monetary sup port, you will want to consider that same community in terms of its capacity to spend money. Your board should ask the fol-lowing questions to understand your community from a purely quantitative perspective:

- What is the size of the market in terms of residential popu-lation and local businesses?
- What is the demographic background in terms of age, gen-der, educational level, income, and other considerations?

This information is publicly available via census records and provides a bird's-eye view of the community at a statistical level. I find that is it especially useful for earned revenue because you are interested in understanding your community as a revenue-bearing market. For an example, see the chart in figure 3.1 by Max van Balgooy of Engaging Places, LLC, which he created for the Haas-Lilienthal House in San Francisco. In the chart, van Balgooy created a system for understanding the various residen-tial subtypes of the area, segmented by geographic distance from the site. The creation and analysis of such information can help you understand the structure, priorities, and means of your community.

Figure 3.1.   Audience Composition Chart. Max A. van Balgooy, Engaging Places LLC, courtesy of San Francisco Heritage

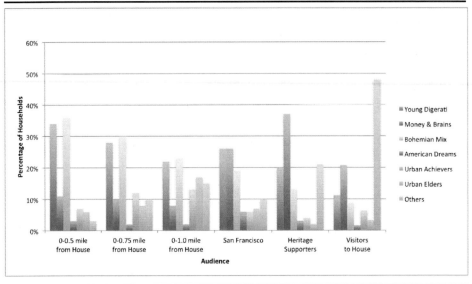

Next, you want to consider more qualitative information, the "how" and "what" of the area:

- What other nonprofit organizations are in the region?
- How do they earn money? How successful are those actions, and how do you define success (attendance, earnings, positive word-of-mouth)?
- What offerings could your community make use of that are not currently available?
- Could your site be a resource to the community? How specifically?

The last question is an important one as you consider earned revenue. The utilization of a historic site for public purposes is—and should be—focused on history and educational value. The site does not exist in a vacuum and can be responsive to public

of opportunities to grow admissions as your organization evolves, and this element of earned revenue should not remain static. Be ready to come back to your admissions structure and advertising after six months or so, and then on an annual basis to update as necessary.

Tours and Ticketed Events

You may elect to offer tours inclusive with general admission, which is typical of many sites. If so, be sure to articulate to your visitors if the tours are self-guided or led by guides, and which areas of the site are open for exploration by visitors and which are not (those spaces that are off-limits should be labeled as such). Tours can also be a great opportunity to welcome visitors outside of your general admissions structure. The simplest example is tours available for students, such as tours available for school groups based on curricular needs. Such tours can be given at a discounted rate, especially if you aim to grow your relationship with students, families, and the educational institutions themselves.

Tours can, however, be major money earners for your site. Be open to offering behind-the-scenes tours, or specialized tours that are available only for a limited time, such as seasonal holiday tours. Specialized tours may be available for private reservation, or only at certain times of the year. Seasonal tours are perhaps more time-consuming to organize, but they can garner high attendance and the opportunity to showcase your site in different ways. If you incorporate regular special tours in your schedule, they can augment your general admissions income as well as serve as a sustainable form of engagement. Your constituency may grow to anticipate your holiday tour with the house fully decorated for the season, or your summer tour of the gardens (after which you serve strawberry shortcake on the veranda). An example of website promotion for special tours of Mount Vernon is included in figure 3.2.

* * *

Case Study: Montgomery History[3]
Rockville, Maryland

Mission: The Montgomery County Historical Society collects, inter-
prets, and promotes the history, heritage and culture of Montgomery
County, Maryland.[4]

In 1815, Montgomery County Clerk Upton Beall and his family
moved into a recently constructed Federal-style house in Rockville, Maryland. His family resided in the house for generations,
with residents including a female cousin who married a farmer
by the name of John Dawson, hence the Beall-Dawson moniker
that the structure holds today. The house remained in the family
for over 130 years, until it was sold to the Davis family in 1946,
who in turn sold it to the City of Rockville in 1965.

The Montgomery County Historical Society was founded in
1944, and until the mid-1960s had functioned as an independent
organization. The Historical Society formally joined with the
City of Rockville when the city purchased the Beall-Dawson
House, and the house soon became the headquarters of the Historical Society. Together with the City, the Society still manages
the house, as well as a museum, library, and administrative
office on the site. In 1972, the circa-1850 medical office of Dr.
Edward E. Stonestreet was donated to the Montgomery County
Historical Society, and the complex grew to include the building
as the Stonestreet Museum of 19th-Century Medicine. The society realized its current iteration in 1993 with the renovation of a
property garage into the Jane C. Sweeen Library.

In October 2015, the site underwent rebranding to shake the
"elitist" and "static" reputation it had experienced as a historical
society and to energize visitation, and reemerged with a new
name: Montgomery History.[5] In a bold move, staff members
decided to remove the furniture that had constituted a decades-
long period interpretation of the Beall-Dawson House, the inten-
tion to free the space for more and rotating exhibitions of the 95
percent of the collection that rarely saw exhibition, specifically

the large collection of textiles stored in the attic. When the textiles were moved, however, staff members discovered a widespread infestation of carpet beetles. Proper conservation ensured that each individual textile be frozen to terminate the infestation and examined for damage.

Instead of allowing the infestation to be a discouraging setback, the collections team at Montgomery History, led by curator Elizabeth Mowll Lay, embraced the challenge as a unique opportunity for visitor engagement. The team constructed an ad hoc artifact inspection laboratory in the Beall-Dawson House, in which for a $10–15 ticket price (up from typical admission rates of $3 for children and $5 for adults), visitors could observe in a weekly special tour the freezing process (in a standard household refrigerator) and inspection of the individual objects by collections staff. The project benefited from promotion by the Smithsonian Associates program, which increased attendance by advertising the tours to its fifty thousand–member mailing list.

Today, Montgomery History continues to enjoy regular collaboration with Smithsonian Associates, as well as special programming hosted in collaboration with other organizations like the Art Deco League of Washington, D.C., and the Society of American Furniture Makers. The program has provided for an increase in attendance, which Lay estimates since 2014 to have grown 60 percent for general attendance and 90 percent for adult attendance specifically, has provided for a sustainable engagement program, and has illustrated a need that positions Montgomery History for an upcoming capital campaign.

What can we learn?

- Embrace challenges. The carpet beetle infestation may ring true with many readers who have experienced a collections challenge that seemed too internal to appeal to the outside world. Yet, welcoming visitors behind the curtain and into the conservation process engaged visitors in such a way that created an income stream from tour ticket sales and laid the groundwork for the needs to be funded in through donations via a capital campaign.

- Be flexible and willing to adapt to new opportunities. Lay explains that though small museums may be limited in many ways, it is easier for smaller organizations to react to good press and take advantage of proposed collaborations and innovative offerings.

Another element of your income structure may be ticketed events. I purposely separate ticketed events from specialized tours because they can be built in a number of ways, whether around a tour or not. Concerts, themed social gatherings, dinners, and many more options can serve to increase visitation and admissions income, and such offerings can also attract audiences that you may not have reached otherwise. Many house museums are exploring unique programming to reach markets with which house museums have historically struggled—such as young professionals—and realizing success in terms of revenue and visitor engagement.

* * *

Case Study: Alexander Ramsey House[6]
St. Paul, Minnesota

Mission: Using the power of history to transform lives, the Minnesota Historical Society is a nonprofit educational and cultural institution established in 1849. The society preserves our past, shares our state's stories, and connects people with history. It does this through educational programs, historical sites throughout the state and book publishing through the Minnesota Historical Society Press.[7]

The Alexander Ramsey House is the former residence of Alexander Ramsey, the first governor of Minnesota Territory and the second governor of the state of Minnesota. Designed by Minnesota-based architect Monroe Sheire and constructed between 1868 and 1872 for Ramsey and his family, the house remained in the family until the death of Ramsey's last grandchild, Anita, in 1964. At that point, the house and all its contents were left to the Minnesota Historical Society, who successfully applied to list the house on the National Register of Historic

Places in 1969. Today, the Alexander Ramsey House is one of twenty-six historic sites and museums stewarded by the Minnesota Historical Society, and its programming focuses on Victorian life in the city of St. Paul. Income is earned via tour admissions, especially around the holiday season when the site holds holiday tours, and the Carriage House Gift Shop, which has historically not been a high earner.[8]

By 2008, the Alexander Ramsey House was in danger of closing. Budget cuts had led to a decrease in staff and in public hours, and according to Minnesota Historical Society Community Engagement Specialist Rachel Abbott, the house was in a funk.[9] Their breadth of their extensive collection, bequeathed by the Ramsey family, had become an albatross, stifling interpretation with space limitations. To implement change, the Minnesota Historical Society contracted a firm that specializes in audience research and strategic initiatives, which surveyed visitors and found that people were bored with staid museum tours.[10] In reaction, staff reinterpreted the house to embrace its original use as a social domestic space, as it had served the Ramseys. Informal gatherings replaced structured tours; a highlight includes History Happy Hours, a ticketed event in which drinks are served and historical topics are the focus of casual discussion among attendees.[11] Abbott explained in a 2014 interview with Minnesota Public Radio that they found success outside the traditional guided tour structure:

> If you have a kitchen, how can you make food in it, how can you let people smell food in it? If you have a playroom, is there a way to let kids play with toys in there? If you have a parlor, can you have social programs where it feels like the space is being used the way it was originally intended?[12]

The technique resonated with audiences, and by 2013, earned revenue at the Ramsey House had jumped from 27 percent of its annual income to 66 percent of the budget. An endowment was established in 2012, the success of which owed to the mission-enhanced programming that engages individuals and encourages support.[13] Today, the Alexander Ramsey House has a robust programming schedule that attracts approximately thirteen thousand visitors per year.

What can we learn?

- Preparation for launching new initiatives, including but not at all limited to earned revenue streams, is imperative. By surveying their audience, the staff of the Alexander Ramsey House was able to launch innovative programming that was immediately impactful.
- Think outside the box as you consider how to distinguish yourself from other sites that follow more traditional methods. Innovative programming informed by strategic planning and audience research beckons press, visitors, and earned revenue.

* * *

Sale of Goods

One of the most common forms of earned income is via sales, usually in the structure of a gift shop. The museum gift shop is a popular earned revenue activity and is popular for a number of reasons: many visitors expect to spend a bit of money in a gift shop whenever they visit a museum; a gift shop provides the opportunity to sell branded items and thus expand your promotional reach; and the sales are immediate transactions, with payment received onsite.[14]

Challenges of a shop are not insurmountable and worth thinking about ahead of time. Whichever objects you choose to purchase for resale, commission, or order specifically for your store, the mission must be a part of the decision-making process. You're keeping UBIT in mind, of course, but also thinking about how you are cultivating an image of goods in keeping with that of your museum.[15] Are there local artisans with whom you can work to display their wares for commission? Are there scholarly and popular publications you want to offer for students and scholars? How do the objects you wish to sell create and contribute to a cohesive theme: do they speak to history in general? A certain region or historical event?

In addition to considering the purchases for resale from a strategic and content-specific perspective, also remember to be cognizant of inventory control. Consider how to price objects so that you can successfully sell them to customers and at a profit. Prices should be determined that account for the wholesale price of any objects you purchase for resale, but you also want any prices to reflect the indirect costs incurred by the shop: utilities cost to keep the lights on and any staff time dedicated to shop management—including behind-the-scenes tasks should as recordkeeping—should be offset by income. Make sure that the sale prices are determined according to resale costs and these indirect costs as well, ideally with money coming in that won't immediately need to pay expenses. Though you are nonprofit, overhead expenses and management of expectations must be properly documented.

Along these same lines, inventory control is important. I recommend starting small, with a few items that customers may expect when they visit the site. Publications of interest to residents and tourists, children's educational resources, and a couple of simple, branded goods, such as postcards, are both inexpensive to acquire, can be ordered in small batches, and are sure to generate sales. For the purposes of UBIT, if that is a concern, remember that low-cost items are not taxable if they promote the site or a broader educational message (or both). If in doubt, follow the example set by many museum stores, in which a label is affixed to the price tag and literally explicates the educational value, such as the historical relevance, of an item for sale.

Another thing to keep in mind is the physical placement of the store. This question has been ongoing for quite some time in the museum world: should a store be in the museum, available only to those who have paid admission, or should it be accessible to the general public and not just museum visitors? In small museums situated in historic sites, the choice of location may be

Figure 3.2.   Mount Vernon Events Page. Courtesy of Mount Vernon Ladies' Association

made for you based on the space available. For most historic sites and houses, admissions and the gift store can be in the same location without asserting too much pressure on the visitor. Such a setup is often borne of necessity, and it does encourage visitors to become customers.

Perhaps you do not yet have the means or the space to set up a physical store, which is quite typical. You do want to try to have a shop open during your hours of admission, which can sometime strain your staff or volunteer resources and not be a feasible option for a new site in its earliest phase. You may wish to think about offering sales online as well as in your brick-and-mortar location. There is no minimum (or limit!) to the number of items to offer for sale, and you can reach a greater customer

PRIVATE EVENING TOUR OPTIONS

Step back in time to walk in George Washington's footsteps and enjoy lantern lit lanes at Mount Vernon. Your extraordinary evening may include a personalized candlelight tour of the Mansion with stunning Potomac River views, a look at the fascinating Distillery & Gristmill, or an entertaining experience in the Museum and Education Center.

GEORGE WASHINGTON'S MANSION

Enjoy exclusive access to the most popular historic home in America.

Cost: $35 per guest; $1,000 minimum ($30 per guest for groups of 100 or more)

GEORGE WASHINGTON'S DISTILLERY & GRISTMILL

Tour a fully-functional reconstruction of George Washington's innovative distillery and gristmill.

Cost: $25 per guest; $1,000 minimum

DONALD W. REYNOLDS MUSEUM AND EDUCATION CENTER

Explore 23 galleries, interactive displays, an immersive movie experience, and a rich and comprehensive collection of more than 700 artifacts.

Cost: $20 per guest; $1,000 minimum

TOUR ENHANCEMENTS

Customize your exclusive experience by adding one or more of the following tour enhancements to your primary tour option on the left.

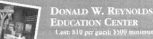

We Fight To Be Free
Action Adventure Movie (18 minutes)
Cost: $5 per guest; $300 minimum

DONALD W. REYNOLDS EDUCATION CENTER
Cost: $10 per guest; $500 minimum*

DONALD W. REYNOLDS MUSEUM
Cost: $10 per guest; $500 minimum*

*Enjoy access to either the Museum or Education Center for just $10 per person, or $15 for both.

PEOPLE FROM THE PAST
Invite a character from Washington's era to join your group as you tour the Estate or enjoy dinner at the Mount Vernon Inn.
Prices range from $400 - $1,200 per performance

base than that achieved only from foot traffic. If you are reluctant to handle online transactions, consider having a webpage devoted to items for sale with an order form for printing or a phone number to call to place an order, which is absolutely acceptable as you're getting started. See figure 3.3 for a sample order form from Montgomery History.

Finally, don't forget that it is perfectly legal for you to sell goods off-site as well. Perhaps you plan to host a collaborative event at another site, or you have a steward, such as a municipal Town Hall or a university, with whom you have negotiated an arrangement to sell goods at an off-site location. I worked with an organization in the past that sold books about local history at the neighborhood independent bookstore for a shared profit. As long as any negotiations are well documented, I encourage sales at off-site or shared locations. Such arrangements can serve as a platform for audience-building promotion as well as potential sales opportunities that require little manpower.

Rental Events

One of the most common ways for historic house museums to earn income is via private rentals. These are events that are not open to the public but rather those for which the site serves as a venue. Private rental activity can range from regular rentals to local businesses and organizations for meeting space, all the way to special event rentals for weddings and parties. Historic sites can be quite successful in soliciting private rental clients because they often have unique and attractive facilities that make for a pleasing setting.

If you are interested in pursuing private rentals, you must be well prepared to invest time in your rental clients. You should be ready to invest in the endeavor financially, for paid advertising is necessary to promote the use of the house as a venue. Your website should include professional photography of the site, and you may wish to advertise in local and regional publications (such as wedding magazines), and your website itself should be informational and illustrative of the site's potential and flexibility for different event types. Consider taking photographs of rooms set up for business meetings, speakers and lectures, and parties to show the different uses one can make of the site.

If you have a site that you believe would be ideal for private rentals, there are a number of preparatory documents to draft, share with your board, and eventually disseminate to potential clients. Those materials may consist of any of the following:

- Rental Guidelines. It is vital before you commit to sharing the house with private rental clients that you draft your rental guidelines. Many sites share such parameters and rules on their website, which is a great way to share basic information and have the resource readily available for potential clients. Make sure to address the following in your guidelines:

- What areas of the site are available for rental: are there certain floors of the house available for rent, or certain areas that are off limits to the public? Can a renter have access to exterior spaces as well?
- Staffing expectations. Will you have a staff member on site during the event? What role will that person serve: to act solely as staff representative, or in a more participatory capacity in the event?
- Catering. Will you allow hot and cold food service? Will you allow all beverages (many historic houses restrict red wine and colored drinks for fear of stains)? Is there a preferred caterer list of firms with whom you are comfortable, such as those with insurance and their own liquor license? Are there adequate food preparation facilities available onsite?
- Amenities. Is there a dressing room available for the wedding party (that is, if you plan to offer the site as a wedding venue)? Is there a separate entrance for the caterer? A coatroom? Multiple bathrooms? Chairs, tables, and other furniture?
- Decorations. Will you allow decorations to be taped or tacked to surfaces? Will you allow confetti, glitter, or any other loose pieces of decoration? Will you allow candles?
- Cleaning. Will the house be fully cleaned before and after events? Who will take out the trash? Who will pay for such anticipated cleaning, and who will be responsible for paying for any additional cleaning needs incurred during the rental?
- Film and Photography Policies. Such a policy may be a part of your rental guidelines, or may be separate. You want to address these topics:
  - Is flash photography allowed throughout the rental area?

Figure 3.3.   Montgomery History Book List. Elizabeth Lay, Curator, Montgomery History

Museum Shop

The Beall-Dawson Museum House gift shop is the place to find unique gifts with a hometown twist. This is only a select list, so be sure to visit the shop for even more books and publications to choose from, as well as jewelry, toys, tea, honey and home décor items.

Give the Gift of History
Or you can give the gift that keeps on giving: AN ANNUAL MEMBERSHIP TO Montgomery County Historical Society! Call 301-340-2825 for more information or www.montgomeryhistory.org. All memberships and donations are tax deductible.

LOCAL TOPICS

Send for the Doctor: The Life and Times of Dr. E. Stonestreet *Clarence R. Hickey. $18*

A Grateful Remembrance: The Story of Montgomery County *Richard McMaster and Ray Eldon Herbert $16.95*

Atlas of Fifteen Miles Around Washington Including the County of Montgomery Maryland, 1879. *Compiled Compiled by G.M. Hopkins $7*

Circling Historic Landscapes, 2nd ed. *Edited by Margaret Coleman. $20*

History of Montgomery County, Maryland: Earliest Settlement In 1650-1879 *T.H.S. Boyd $19.50*

Maryland A New Guide to the Old Line State *Earl Arnett and Robert Brugger $35*

Uncle Tom's Cabin *Harriet Beecher Stowe $20.95*

The Met: 125 Years of the Metropolitan Branch Of the B&O Railroad *Susan Cooke Soderberg $8*

Lilly Stone *Judith Welles $15*

From Slave Ship to Harvard *James H Johnston $32*

Maryland Ghosts *Dorothy Pugh and Karen Lottes $19.99*

Seth *William Offutt $29.95*

Wild Women of Maryland *Lauren Silberman $21.99*

Mama Wears Two Aprons: *Women in Aprons: Women in Farming and Farm Marketing Margaret Coleman $15*

Montgomery County *Michael Dwyer $22*

Civil War Guide to Montgomery County *Charles Jacobs $15*

TOWNS AND COMMUNITIES

Trembling in the Balance: The Chesapeake & Ohio Canal During the Civil War *Timothy Snyder $22.95*

Discovering the C&O Canal *Mark Sabatke $27*

History of Germantown, Maryland *Susan Soderberg $10*

Small Town in the Big City, Story of Chevy Chase *Peggy Fleming, Joanne Zich $24.95*

Gaithersburg Then and Now *Shaun Curtis. $21.99*

Glen Echo Park: The Remarkable Saga of a Very Small Town *Carlotta Anderson $15*

History of Hyattstown *Dona Cuttler, Michael Dwyer $12*

Cabin John: Legends and Life of an UnCommon Place Judith Welles. $17

Somerset: One Hundred Years a Town Lesley Ann Simmons with Donna Kathleen Harman. $20

Latinos in the Washington DC area Maria Sprehn $21.99

Rockville's Recent Past Teresa Lachin $12

More towns and community books available in the shop!

Rockville: Portrait of a City Eileen S. McGuckian $42.95

Forest Glen Rich Schaeffer and Ric Nelson $19.99

Wheaton Laura Leigh Palmer $20

Takoma Park: Portrait of a Victorian Suburb Ellen R. Marsh and Mary Anne O'Boyle $30

Historic Silver Spring (Images of America) Jerry McCoy $22

OUR MARYLAND HERITAGE William Neal Hurley, Jr.

A series of histories of families found primarily in Montgomery County and Maryland. Each book provides general information about a principal family and an index listing names of individuals by marriage. This is a sampling; more family names available in the shop.

Book 2: The Walker Families $20.50
Book 5: The King Families $38
Book 8: The Brandenburg Families $22
Book 11: The Stottlemyer Families $18
Book 12: The Browning Families $45.50
Book 14: The Lewis Families $37
Book 15: The Warfield Families $21.50
Book 18: The Young Families $21.50
Book 19: The Bowman & Gue Families $19.50
Book 21: The Fisher and Beckwith Families $20
Book 22: The Davis Families $26.00
Book 24: The Holland Families $22.50
Book 26: The Trail Families $22

Book 25: The Rickett Families $21
Book 27: The Rabbit Families $16.50
Book 28: The Baker Families $24
Book 31: The Hays and Gott Families $18
Book 32: The Waters Family $33.50
Book 33: The Griffith Families $28
Book 35: The Benson Families $16
Book 37: The Higgins Families $19
Book 38: The Shaw Families $17.50
Book 40: The Nicholson Families $17
Book 42: The Cashell and Plummer Families $20.50
Book 43: The Hilton Family $25

MAPS AND MISCELLANEOUS

1865 Martinet & Bond Map –$15
Detailed with land owners and structures

Civil War Troop Movements Map $15

Beall Dawson Tea $6

Bicentennial Map of Montgomery County Maryland $15

Genealogy Family Trees $4

Montgomery County Historical Society Notecards - Beall Dawson and interior of the Stonestreet Museum of the 19th century medicine – 6 of each $14

Barns of Mont Cty, MD Box of 12 $6

MUSEUM SHOP BOOKS NOT LISTED HERE INCLUDE:
Genealogy, Maryland, Washington D.C., African-American history, Civil War, local folklore, books for children and more. Please stop by and browse our selection.

Many of the books listed here have limited availability. To be certain the book you want is in stock please call 301-340-2825. The shop is located at 103 West Montgomery Avenue Rockville, MD 20850 and is open Wednesday through Sunday from 12-4.

- Are there particular photographers knowledgeable about the site that you encourage clients to work with?
- Will the representatives of the site be able to take photographs and/or share photography for promotional purposes?
- Site Visual Resources. The aforementioned photography of a variety of rental types is recommended, as is a floor plan of areas available for rental.
- Other Rental Considerations. Many sites have particular needs that they must communicate to clients. You should check with your local municipality regarding alcohol service permits, as well as use permits if your site is in a designated park. Also be prepared to share information regarding compliance with the Americans with Disabilities Act, such as elevator, threshold, and ramp availability and specifications. Including this information on both event and admissions pages of your website is recommended.
- Agreement. The rental agreement that you draft and review with potential renters should review all guidelines and outline payment details. Liability and other responsibilities should also be outlined in the document. This will function as your contract, so you will want to have clients return a signed and dated copy along with payment. I recommend requiring a down payment to confirm and hold the date, with final payment due no later than the date of the event. See figure 3.4 for a sample rental agreement.

It may be no surprise looking at these recommendations, but so much of the work of private rentals is handling client expectations while also managing risks. For every possible question I have encouraged you to answer in your guidelines, there will be ten more situations that make you scramble to update your policies. I will take this opportunity to tell you that is completely normal: simply be prepared to dedicate time to policy review and revision. Likewise, much time should be budgeted for client interactions. The agreement you offer clients should protect your site and communicate expectations, but will also commit your organization to providing certain services. Consider including in your policy your open hours and the number of planning meetings anticipated in advance of the event.

Archives

One form of revenue that is often overlooked: you might have as a resource a collection of objects or of historical records, such as those related to past residents of the site, the region, or an event of historical significance. If and when your records have been properly archived and organized, these are valuable educational and historical resources that you can make available to the general public. While some sites do offer access and research services for free, I encourage you to formalize a policy of research for a fee, which serves two purposes: first, it provides an additional avenue of earned revenue; second, such a system controls and documents your interactions with the public regarding research requests. A structure, which can and should be advertised on your website, allows you to track requests and to manage them efficiently. The Maine Historical Society offers a good example, available in figure 3.5.

Just as with events, archival research can be a serious commitment of staff or volunteer resources. By stating your offerings with associated costs, you are properly valuing the internal time necessary to commit to such work and creating a professional platform for such work to be conducted for the public. There are multiple ways to build a fee structure for archival work, which can consist of a flat fee per research request, a cost per reproduced page or photograph, or an hourly rate for professional research services or archival access. To promote the educational value of the collections, you may choose to exempt students or teachers from such a fee. Or, if you wish to promote membership, a discount could be offered with a new membership. Regardless of the specific discretion you exercise regarding your audience and the services to offer, just remember to properly value your services.

Figure 3.4.   Sample Rental Contract.

SAMPLE RENTAL APPLICATION AND AGREEMENT

Renter: _____

Organization: _____

Address: _____

City: _____ State: _____ Zip: _____

Telephone: _____ Email: _____

Is this a Town or Non-profit organization? Yes:_____ No: _____
(Please be prepared to show documentation)

Type of Activity: Event _____ Meeting _____

Date(s) Requested: _____ Time In: _____ Time Out: _____

Expected Attendance: _____

Will Alcohol Be Served?   _____

Fees:

Meeting Rates:
Non-Town Resident: $100/hour
Resident: $75/hour
Nonprofit/Town Business: $75/hour

        Minimum Meeting Rental: 2 hours

Event Rates:
Non-Town Resident: $175/hour
Resident: $125/hour
Nonprofit/Town Business: $125/hour

        Minimum Event Rental: 4 hours

Custodial Fee: $75/rental
Energy Surcharge (November 1st-April 30th): $20/hour

Rules and Regulations:

1. No tape, nails, glue, pins or paint of any type may be used for decorating or any other purpose in the facility.
2. This is a "no smoking" facility. No smoking of any products is allowed on the premises.
3. Only the furniture available for rental use may be moved. No furniture, fixtures, or equipment is to be removed from the building.

MHS Research Request Form (or fill out **online** at www.mainehistory.org/research)

Patron Information

Member # _____ Date of Request _____

Name: _____

Address: _____

Email: _____

Phone: _____

Payment Information (advanced payment required)

Card type (circle one) VISA   MasterCard   Discover   Pay by Check

Card Number: _____Exp_____

Name as it appears on card: _____

Signature: _____

Research Request (use separate page if necessary)

• List the specific question(s) you wish answered or your general research request
• Provide all information you have concerning the individual(s) you wish researched
• List the sources you have already searched
• Use the space below or attach a letter of explanation

_____
_____
_____
_____
_____

Research is conducted at the rates indicated on the reverse of this form. Results may be sent via mail or email. Shipping charges are $3.50 for U.S. locations. Digitization costs may apply for lengthy PDFs.

I authorize _____ **hours of research.** (Maximum of 5 hours) You will only be charged for the hours used.
                        Signature _____

Select the research you are requesting:

__In-depth research

__Photocopy service

__Quick Search

Maine Historical Society
Library Research Services

Maine Historical Society
Brown Research Library
489 Congress Street
Portland, Maine 04101-3498
(207) 774-1822
research@mainehistory.org
www.mainehistory.org/research

Hours:
10 am to 4 pm
Tuesday through Saturday
May - October
Wenesday through Saturday
November - April

Earned Revenue Evaluation

As with all other strategic initiatives, you want to make sure to create a structure for evaluation of your activity. Make time, perhaps quarterly, to analyze your earned revenue activities and determine their value versus investment. Consider approaching evaluation according to at least three areas:

• Investment. How are you seeing a return on your investment? Are you earning income, enough to cover activity-related expenditures? Are you growing visitation, membership, and contributed income? How are you managing costs and staff time investment, and is there anything you could do to make your operation more efficient or productive?[16]

Figure 3.5.   *Maine Historical Society Research Form. Collection of Maine Historical Society*

Maine Historical Society Brown Library Research Services

We invite you to visit our facility to take advantage of our holdings but sometimes that might not fit into your schedule. For those of you unable to
visit the Library, we offer various categories of research—family history, general Maine history, historic homes. Use the Research Request form
on our website at www.mainehistory.org/research and include credit card information. MHS members will receive a 10% discount.

Service:	Fees:	Examples:
Photocopy Service Copy service for a specific number of photocopies from a known source. (Copyright and other considerations prevent photocopying entire books and original manuscripts.)	$10.00 per source Includes up to 5 photocopies Additional photocopies at $.25 each 25 page maximum	• Please send me a copy of the Rufus King Libby family that begins on page 164 of *The Libby family in America.*
Quick Search Searching an obvious source for a specific question requiring less than 15 minutes.	$15.00 per request Includes up to 5 photocopies Additional photocopies at $.25 each	• Was John Jones living in Portland in 1930?
In-depth Research Research for open-ended questions involving a number of sources.	$40.00 per hour with a maximum of 5 hours at a time Up to 5 photocopies included Additional photocopies at $.25 each	• My great grandfather was living in Eastport in 1850. Can you tell me his siblings and parents?
Imaging Services and Permission to publish	*Digital reproductions of images from our collections* *www.VintageMaineImages.com*	
Ready-reference	*No charge. Phone or email requests accepted.*	

Visit our websites:
www.MaineHistory.org - Website of the Maine Historical Society
www.MaineMemory.net - Maine's digital museum, archive and educational resource
www.VintageMaineImages.com - The place to purchase digital reproductions of historical images from Maine

---

- Engagement. Are you filling a need in your community? Are you benefiting your community and growing your market? Are there opportunities for feedback? If not, how will you solicit it, and if so, how will you address it?
- Income. How does the income your venture generates offset implementation costs? If the activity is not currently making money, what time frame will you work within before you consider changing course?

Conclusion

This chapter has introduced the basic avenues of earned revenue such as admissions, tours and events, sales, and research. Start simple and allow yourself time to grow, to plan adequately for

4. Artwork will not be touched.
5. The fireplaces are not to be used.
6. Any use of candles must be approved by the Executive Director.
7. Children under 18 must be supervised at all times.
8. Events are limited to the first floor and no guests are allowed on the upper floors during private rentals.
9. Alcoholic beverages are only allowed under the following guidelines:
   a. The serving of alcohol is handled by an insured professional who can present a Certificate of Liability.
   b. A one-day liquor license is filed with and approved by the Town. Please allow two weeks before your rental date for processing.
   c. On days of regular education sessions, alcohol consumption is only allowed at least one hour following the end of school hours.
10. The serving of any food items must be approved by the Town Health Department and, if necessary, a Catering Permit must be issued.
11. Parking availability is not guaranteed and on occasion may be limited. Please plan accordingly
12. The House is subject to curfew mandated by the Town. Hours of public use must take place by 10:00 PM Sunday through Thursday and by 11:00 PM on Fridays and Saturdays.
13. The House reserves the right to adjust any regulations where health and safety of any event participant is affected before, during, or after the event.

Liability Statement:

By signing this rental agreement, the rental client agrees to assume the responsibility and legal liability for the above-described event and to abide by all rules and regulations. The renter agrees to indemnify, defend and hold harmless the Town and the Historical Society and their officers, employees, and agents from any and all claims of action, liability, judgments, costs, and expenses, including attorney fees and claims for bodily injury or property damages that may arise out of or in connection with this agreement and its use. Failure to comply with any or all of the above stated rules will result in the withholding of the security deposit. Any physical damage to the House during private rental is the sole responsibility of the client.

I certify that I have read and understood the rules and regulations and shall accept responsibility on behalf of myself and all event participants for any damage or theft sustained by the House in the course of the event referenced above.

Signature: _____ Date: _____

Approved By: _____ Date: _____

Please contact (xxx) xxx-xxxx or director@xxxxx.org with any questions.

We wish you a pleasant event and hope you enjoy use of the House!

earned revenue activities and to execute and evaluate these plans properly. And don't be afraid to collaborate, to have fun, and to try new things! Too often, historic house museums are maligned for subsisting on admissions and shop sales, their operation whittled down to a skeleton crew of volunteers in a dusty house. Unique earned income ventures can be the key to self-sufficiency and sustainability. And now that we have discussed contributed income and earned revenue, let's move to the other side of the balance sheet in the next chapter: expenses, budgets, and financial management.

Key Points: Checklist

Along with contributed income, earned revenue is a vital support stream for all nonprofit organizations, including historic sites. This chapter has provided an introduction to earned revenue and the preparation for and explanation of common avenues of earned income, as well as how to evaluate your earned income activities. Here is a checklist of the major points of the chapter for review:

- Planning
  - Market Evaluation
  - Resource Assessment
- Implementation
  - Admissions
    - School Tours
    - Group and Specialized Tours
  - Sales
    - Brick-and-Mortar Store
    - Online Sales
    - Off-site Sales
  - Private Rentals
  - Archival and Research Activities
- Evaluation Considerations
  - Investment
  - Engagement
  - Income

Notes

1. See "Publication 598: Tax on Unrelated Business Income of Exempt Organizations" (Rev. January 2015) for more information. Available from https://www.irs.gov/pub/irs-pdf/p598.pdf.

2. I use the example of a café for a specific reason. Since it is not particularly educational in value, one may ask if it is reasonable to seek revenue from a café or a cafeteria. Such offerings are considered exempt from UBIT under the "convenience exemption," as long as they are not accessible to the general public.

3. Interview with Elizabeth Mowll Lay, Curator.

4. www.montgomeryhistory.org.

5. Elizabeth Mowll Lay, personal communication, December 19, 2016.

6. Interview with Rachel Abbott, Community Engagement Specialist.

7. Minnesota Historical Society, mnhs.org.

8. Rachel Abbott, "New Ideas, Same Old House: Public Feedback, Change and the Alexander Ramsey House," Washington, D.C.: American Alliance of Museums, 2012, 1.

9. Ibid.

10. Rachel Abbott, personal communication, December 20, 2016.

11. Rupa Shenoy, "Happy Hour with the Historical Society," *MPR News*, Minnesota Public Radio, June 15, 2012.

12. Dan Kraker, "Ok to Touch? Glensheen, Home Museums Rethink Rules to Lure Visitors," *MPR News*, Minnesota Public Radio, August 11, 2014.

13. Rachel Abbott, personal communication, December 20, 2016.

14. The sense of place created by museums and the stores that provide support are responsible for creating visitor expectations, according to Haley Shapley in her article, "Exhibit A: The Museum Store," *Gift Shop* (Winter 2011).

15. For a discussion of UBIT in relation to gift shops, see Cinnamon Catlin-Legutko and Stacy Klinger, eds., *Small Museum Toolkit 2: Financial Resource Development and Management* (Lanham, MD: AltaMira Press, 2012), 48.

16. For additional reading on strategic planning and evaluation of earned revenue activities, see Douglass W. McDonald, "Earned Revenue and Investment Income" in *Slaying the Financial Dragon: Strategies for Museums* (Washington, D.C.: American Alliance of Museums, 2003), 69.

4

The Door Swings Both Ways

Managing Income and Expenses

Now that you are in the position as an incorporated 501(c)(3) to receive contributions and to earn income, you will want to situate yourself to prepare for expenses and accurately record financial activity. In this chapter, we will focus on the basic preparatory measures to take and the structures of accounting to get you started.

A word of encouragement: if you are daunted by the concept of accounting—perhaps you have never received formal training—you are far from alone. Have you managed a household budget? Have you ever set up a plan for what you spend on basic expenses, and kept track of what you spend? Those are the exact tools you need to successfully manage organizational finances. Once you unlock the keys to accounting, whether for individual recordkeeping, for-profit business, or nonprofit organizations, the basic principles are the same. In small organizations such as historic sites, you will most likely have to handle the basics on your own. But I can tell you from experience, it's absolutely worth the time investment to learn how to handle your organizational finances well: not only will your site benefit from sound oversight, you will be a better leader for it. Financial management, as we've previously acknowledged, is simply telling the story of your site using a different language.

As you already know, you want to make sure to have your mission statement and strategic plan in hand before embarking

103

on your financial systems. Your finances should reflect your operational and special project goals and the mission-based work of your organization. There are a few other matters to have decided before drafting financial structures.

Preparation and Principles

The most fundamental way to look at accounting is like this: it provides the means to record income versus expenses. If you have a strong hold on your expenses (the money going out of the organization) as well as your earned and contributed income (the money coming in to the organization), you have all the basic information you need to get started. There are three financial procedures by which to manage your funds:

- Statement of Activity (also called the Income Statement or the Profit and Loss Statement)
- Statement of Position (also called a Balance Sheet)
- Statement of Cash Flow

Together, these three documents provide the insight into your financial situation that would be required by the Internal Revenue Service or external funders, if needed. I also recommend drafting the following as you get started:

- Annual Operating Budget
- Special Project Budgets

Most important for any organization is the operating budget, which should provide a delineated account of all anticipated sources and expenses necessary to maintain operation of the site. I also think it is worthwhile for us to address project budgets, which are quite common for historic sites as they seek funding for projects such as restoration and exhibitions, and aim to manage such projects accurately. In this chapter, we will provide an overview of these five complementary methods for managing your finances. Before drafting any of the aforementioned, I have a few recommendations.

Software

First, decide if you plan to purchase financial management software. Most organizations with whom I have worked recommend QuickBooks. This may be a major expense for an organization in its threadbare first year of incorporation, but such software allows for easy tracking and the creation of reports. It's important to start good accounting practices from the start. Invest in the proper tools and equipment up-front and you might save yourself the headache of transferring an established system later on. This will save you valuable time and will aid in a more seamless financial protocol, especially as you plan for regular annual audits.

Accounting Principles

My second recommendation is to make sure you have a clear understanding of basic accounting standards. When people reference accounting principles, they do not refer to de facto accepted procedures. "Generally Accepted Accounting Principles" (GAAP) is the set of guidelines established by the Financial Accounting Standards Board (FASB) to which organizations must adhere when recording and reporting financial data. These principles ensure compliant and consistent reporting structures. Of most benefit to board members and staff of nonprofit organizations is FAS 117, titled "Financial Statements of Not-for-profit Organizations," available from the FASB website.[1] As publicly supported organizations of which the financial statements are available for public dissemination, historic museums must adhere to the standard structure and expectations for reporting information. This consistency proves useful for market comparisons and trends.

Accounting and Bookkeeping Services

Though an obvious goal is to keep expenses to a minimum as you officially begin operation, you will want to formalize a relationship with an accounting firm, preferably one with nonprofit experience. Knowledge of historic structures and land is ideal, since they can provide advisement on how to best document your tangible assets. I recommend asking colleagues in similar organizations in the region with whom they contract for such services. Word-of-mouth among fellow nonprofits, particularly in the art and history sectors, is valuable here, for you want to set up a lasting relationship. An accounting firm will be responsible for reviewing your financial statements and filing your Internal Revenue Service Form 990 and meeting applicable state requirements. Though not required, an accountant can also provide valuable insight and responses to questions you may have as you instigate the incorporation processes and all that follow.

Likewise, you may want to consider enlisting the services of a bookkeeper. The time commitment required from a contract bookkeeper would be minimal, no more than a few hours a month at most. As you get started, you may have to handle bookkeeping duties on a volunteer basis until a staff member is hired; after that, the staff member would be responsible for bookkeeping. At some point and as your administrative needs grow, you will want a bookkeeper. Not only would this offer necessary financial administration, the aid from a bookkeeper will be better for the creation of a structural system of checks and balances. For instance, at many sites a staff member approves invoices, the bookkeeper processes payables, and the treasurer provides final approval.

Cash vs. Accrual Accounting

Finally, and ideally with the advice of an accountant, you will want to decide if the finances will be documented according to the cash method or the accrual method of accounting. The cash method focuses more on actual cash flow, when actual cash transactions occur, and is less concerned with when revenue is actually earned or expenses actually incurred. An example of the cash method is as follows: you write a check to pay for office supplies and record the expense when the check is written. The cash method is popular with organizations that utilize single-entry bookkeeping and that handle relatively few transactions. Because the method cannot account for promised income or expenses (relevant, for instance, in planning for staff wages and benefits), there are definite limitations to cash accounting. The lack of capability to account for promised or pledged income is especially challenging when considering how to document promised gifts or grants.

The accrual method, on the other hand, is a bit more time-consuming, but allows for better tracking of current and planned transactions. The focus is not on cash flow but on when revenue is actually earned and expenses incurred. Here's the corresponding example regarding office supplies: the expense is not considered a complete transaction when the check is written but when it's recorded; the transaction has been completed when the check is cashed and money has left your account. And similar to an insurance premium, the expense is attributed to the period of the economic activity and is not based on the cash transaction. The only downside is that because cash flow is not automatically documented, the IRS requires a cash flow state-ment in addition to the statement of activity and statement of position. Since you will be totally on top of your finances, how-ever, you will want to draft such a document anyway.

So which to use? The cash method may prove appealing to small operations with minimal transactions, but the accrual method is overwhelmingly popular for the level of detail it pro-vides, as well as the opportunity to document ongoing transac-tions, such as gift pledges and planned expenses. I recommend instituting the accrual method if possible, especially considering the specific needs of historic sites to accurately document ongo-ing projects—such as capital restoration and expansion—as well as paid staff. To further seal the deal, the FASB recommends it for audit completion, and many states require the accrual method.

Financial Management

Whether for a for-profit $2 billion corporation or a nonprofit $200,000 organization, the basic accounting principles are the same. As previously mentioned, three documents detail the financial activity: the statement of activity, the statement of financial position, and the statement of cash flows. I will also introduce the annual operating budget and project budgets, since both are invaluable for financial tracking.

Statement of Financial Activity

The statement of activity, also known as the income statement or profit and loss (P&L) statement is the most utilized of the major accounting documents. Most commonly referred to as the P&L, the income statement literally states the income and the expenditures of an organization and how they relate to each other: a balance, in which your income exactly matches your expenses; a surplus, in which you have an excess of income; or a deficit, which means an excess of expenses. This information is reflected in your net surplus (deficit) line of the P&L.

The two categories of income and expenses offer further detail. The revenue section includes all forms of earned revenue, such as admissions and membership, shop sales, private event earnings, and all other earnings. Also included is contributed income, which may include grants, individual gifts, and any other donations. If your organization holds investments, any income, such as interest, should also be included. On the expense side, all general categories of expenses should be listed, such as salaries and wages, facility maintenance, purchases for resale, marketing, and any other expenses incurred, such as the purchase of office supplies and equipment. Each site is different in terms of their funding and their expenses. What is most important is that you create a P&L that accurately captures organizational activity, is consistent over fiscal periods, and aligns with other financial statements for audit purposes.

The statement of activity is essentially your record of income and how money is spent, providing insight into if and how you are functioning within your means (see figure 4.1). This statement works in tandem with your annual operating budget, the figures of which should be included against your actual expenses (budget vs. actuals). Comparing your anticipated income and expenses against actual activity can help with revising expectations. Many organizations review their P&L monthly or quarterly as a snapshot of financial status.

Statement of Financial Position

Also called a balance sheet, the statement of financial position is a comprehensive record of financial standing. Unlike the statement of activity, which documents the activity over a certain period of time, the statement of financial position provides a higher-level analysis, and reflects the accumulation of all activity since incorporation. While the statement of activity is perfect for

Figure 4.1.   Statement of Activities. Elizabeth Hamilton, reprinted from nonprofitaccountingbasics.com

Show context: History; YTD; Budget; Forecast to year end; Explain variances

ORG NAME Statement of Activities	Prior Year Actual	Current Year to Date	Current Year Budget	% Budget to Date	Year End Forecast	Budget to YE Variance	Notes
Income by source							
Earned Revenue							
Contributed Revenue							A
Released from Restriction (1)							
Total Unrestricted Revenue							
Expenses by function / activity							
Program Expense							B
Development Expense							
Admin Expense							
Total Operating Expense							
NET UNRESTRICTED INCOME							
Separate restricted							
Restricted Contributions							C
Released to Unrestricted							
NET RESTRICTED INCOME							
NET ALL ACTIVITY							
Narrative notes							
Note A (Narrative explanation)							
Note B (Narrative explanation)							
Note C (Narrative explanation)							

tweaking expectations and for forecasting purposes, the statement of position is the best measure of an organization's financial health (see table 4.1). The statement of financial position details assets and liabilities, illustrating what you own (assets) and what you owe (liabilities) at a certain point in time.[2]

You want to be confident in your understanding of assets and liabilities as they relate to a nonprofit organization. An asset is something the organization owns for economic benefit. Cash and cash equivalents, receivables, and inventories are all considered assets. Tangible assets, such as land, buildings, and equipment, as well as intangible assets like goodwill should also be included. If you have any tangible property that you will list as an asset, such as land, make sure to have it appraised and double-check with your accountant so you can accurately document its value.[3] Conversely, liabilities are what obligations the organization owes. This includes payables, borrowings (such as project financing), long-term borrowing (arrangements that exceed one year for planned repayment), and taxes payable, as well as any other operational needs.[4] Programming and fundraising costs should also be included as liabilities, of the transactions are not completed and payment is owed. Net assets or fund balances are the difference between what you own and what you owe. This remainder may be further categorized from unrestricted, which can be used for any needs the organization may have, to temporarily restricted and ultimately permanently restricted, such as endowment funds. The net assets of an organization are essentially the worth of the organization. A consistent increase in net assets means your operation is strong, and a decrease reflects insufficient support to sustain expenses (or that an investment has been made over the fiscal period to strengthen the organization—if so, be sure to explain). These terms will come up regularly as you manage your finances, especially your balance sheet, so make sure you are conversant in the assets and liabilities of your organization.

The most important consideration as you draft and utilize your balance sheet is that your balance sheet must always *balance*. Your total assets will always equal your liabilities plus your net assets.

Table 4.1. Statement of Position. Elizabeth Hamilton, reprinted from nonprofitaccountingbasics.com

ORG NAME Statement of Financial Position as of [DATE]	Total To Date	Current Year		Restricted	Note	Prior Year
		Unrestricted				
		Operations	Board Designated			
ASSETS						
Current Assets	50,000	25,000	15,000	10,000	A	42,000
Fixed Assets	20,000	-	20,000	-		20,750
Long Term Assets	-	-	-	-	B	
TOTAL ASSETS	70,000	25,000	35,000	10,000		62,750
LIABILITIES						
Current Liabilities	3,000	3,000	-	-		3,500
Long Term Liabilities	-	-	-	-		-
TOTAL LIABILITIES	3,000	3,000	-	-		3,500
NET ASSETS						
Unrestricted						
Undesignated	22,000	22,000	-	-		26,500
Board Designated	15,000	-	15,000	-	C	
Property, Plant & Equip	20,000	-	20,000	-		20,750
Temporarily Restricted	10,000	-	-	10,000		12,000
Permanently Restricted	-	-	-	-		
TOTAL NET ASSETS	67,000	22,000	35,000	10,000		59,250
TOTAL LIABILITIES & NET ASSETS	70,000	25,000	35,000	10,000		62,750
Note A (Narrative explanation)						
Note B (Narrative explanation)						
Note C (Narrative explanation)						

Statement of Cash Flows

The last of the three primary financial statements for audit purposes, the statement of cash flows, is required by FAS 117 for all organizations that prepare their finances according to the accrual method. The statement of cash flows accounts for the change in cash and cash equivalents during a financial period, and summarizes the sources and uses of cash during the corresponding period of the statement of activity (P&L) (see figure 4.2). This document is important because it serves as a record of information not readily available in the income statement or the balance sheet, such as repayment of long-term debt, investment activity, or purchase of fixed assets. Cash flow is delineated into the following categories:

- Operating Activity: general administration, such as programming and fundraising
- Investing Activity: purchase/sale of investments, property, plants, or equipment
- Financing Activity: amounts received from borrowings as well as repayments

The statement of cash flows is exactly as it sounds and provides a view of the cash coming in and the cash going out. While the statement of activity shows if you are functioning at a surplus or a deficit, and the statement of position illustrates your overall financial health, the statement of cash flows details how much cash is on hand. This information is especially useful when determining the "days cash on hand," meaning how many days the organization can pay operating expenses with the cash currently available. To know your cash on hand will help you to ensure you have the means by which to handle expenses, which is especially useful to new businesses (including nonprofits) that are not yet generating much income activity, or businesses (including historic sites and museums) that function seasonally.

*   *   *

Figure 4.2. Cash flow template. Reprinted from nonprofitassistancefund.org

Cash on Hand (beginning cash)	0	0	0	0	0	0
RECEIPTS from Support						
Grants - confirmed						
Grants - anticipated						
Individual contributions						
Special events						
Funds released from restricted						
RECEIPTS from Revenue						
Fees at time of service						
Accounts receivable collection						
Rent/facility use						
Ticket sales						
Contract services						
RECEIPTS from other sources						
Loan/Line of credit proceeds						
TOTAL RECEIPTS	0	0	0	0	0	0
DISBURSEMENTS for Operations						
Payroll						
Payroll taxes						
Benefits and staff exp						
TOTAL STAFFING	0	0	0	0	0	0
Rent						
Utilities						
Maintenance, repair						
TOTAL OCCUPANCY	0	0	0	0	0	0
Office exp (phone, postage, supplies)						
Printing and marketing						
Equipment leases						
Insurance						
TOTAL OTHER OPERATING	0	0	0	0	0	0
Legal						
Accounting & audit						
TOTAL PROFESSIONAL SERVICES	0	0	0	0	0	0
TOTAL PROGRAM RELATED	0	0	0	0	0	0
TOTAL OPERATING DISBURSEMENTS	0	0	0	0	0	0
DISBURSEMENTS for Financing						
Mortgage payments						
Loan payments						
Payments on past due obligations						
DISBURSEMENTS for Capital Expenses						
TOTAL DISBURSEMENTS	0	0	0	0	0	0
NET CASH FOR THE PERIOD	0	0	0	0	0	0
ENDING CASH	0	0	0	0	0	0

Case Study: The Bidwell House Museum[5]
Monterey, Massachusetts

Mission: The Bidwell House Museum is a New England heritage site providing a personal encounter with history, early American home life, and the Berkshire landscape through its land, house, and collection. The museum is a nonprofit educational institution for the benefit of the community and today's audiences of all ages, dedicated to preservation, scholarship, and enjoyment of the landmark site.[6]

In 1750, Reverend Adonijah Bidwell was ordained the first minister of Housatonic Township Number One. Sometime in the next decade or so Bidwell and his family moved into their new house, a Georgian, two-story post-and-beam saltbox structure. Bidwell used his house as a parsonage and led services at the nearby meetinghouse for the rest of his life. After Bidwell died in 1784, the settlement moved their meetings to a new space and the property remained in the family, Bidwell's son, also named Adonijah, turning the land into a prosperous dairy farm. The Bidwells sold the farm in 1853 to the Carrington family. The residence was sold to Raymond P. Ensign in 1913, who transitioned the site into the Berkshire Summer School of the Arts. In 1960, designers Jack Hargis and David Brush purchased the site with the goal of restoration to the original era of Adonijah Bidwell's residence. They successfully nominated the site to the National Register of Historic Places in 1982.

Hargis and Brush left the site to a group of friends in the area with the charge to turn the site into a museum. This group formalized as the founding board of directors, and with bequests from Hargis and Brush, opened the site as a museum in 1990. Over the following ten years, the site grew, eventually outsizing the operation that consisted of a sole administrator who also functioned as caretaker of the site. The board had also transitioned over the years, and the board in place in 2004 decided to prioritize professionalization of the site. The first nonresidential executive director arrived in 2005 and in 2009, the site's current director, Barbara Palmer, was hired. Palmer arrived with virtually no experience in financial management beyond that needed to handle household expenses; her back-ground was in publishing and environmental agencies. Undaunted, Palmer solicited meetings with nearby historic site administrators as well as accountants and embarked on an over-haul of the financial management of the site. She excised out-dated code classifications, weeded old invoices and dead projects, and prioritized a new system for money handling using QuickBooks.

Today, the site consists of a historic house, gardens, and trails, all managed by Palmer and two part-time staff members. The Bidwell House Museum is open seasonally between Memo-rial Day and Columbus Day and functions as part of the Historic Berkshires 18th Century Trail, a promotional collaboration between six historic sites in the Berkshires region.

Since conducting her initial financial overhaul, Palmer has hired a part-time bookkeeper to assist in oversight of the $180,000 operation. Earned income consists mainly of tour admissions and earnings from ticketed events such as lectures and workshops, and contributions are solicited via fundraiser events, the annual appeal, and individual gifts, including trustee leadership gifts from board members. Additional revenue comes from investment income, including an unrestricted capital reserve and a restricted, board-designated endowment. Palmer has instituted a regular schedule of financial maintenance that begins with her daily approval of expenses, weekly bookkeeper processing, and monthly reports to the board president and trea-surer. Regular review of budget projections and activity are also analyzed monthly. Quarterly P&L statements are shared with the full board and special projects, such as an ongoing $750,000 capital restoration project, are broken out in complementary Excel spreadsheets generated by QuickBooks. The annual opera-ting budget is drafted in consultation with the board president and treasurer and issued to the full board for discussion and approval.

What can we learn?

- Dive in and seek advice. Palmer had little financial experi-ence when she started, but embraced the opportunity to learn about financial management and how to manage a site well. Her commitment paid off in a well-structured operation.

- Historic house museum professionals are the Swiss-army knives of museum workers—embrace flexibility under conditions of limited resources. As Palmer notes, "The Bidwell House has all the functions of the Metropolitan Museum of Art, just fewer people to do them."[7]

* * *

Annual Operating Budget

No less essential is your annual operating budget, though it is not required by the FASB for annual reporting. Your operating budget is your fundamental action plan for the financial period, and is best created annually, and managed in smaller installments (such as monthly or quarterly) for the purposes of comparing your actual activity to budgeted figures via regular P&L statements. The operating budget should be prepared three to four months in advance of each fiscal year, drafted by staff and reviewed by the finance committee of the board, and then ultimately put to a full board vote for approval. If the organization does not yet have staff, the board should prepare the budget and vote to ensure approval. The involvement of the board is vital in the preparation and execution of the operating budget, for the operating budget should reflect priorities and help board members face strategic issues and acknowledge resource constraints in a timely manner.

Initial financial planning will consist of drafting an operating budget, which will in turn inform your other documents. The operating budget should reflect all activities for the coming year by line item, with each line item supported by details that can be broken out, if necessary. For instance, let's say you have a printing and publication line item that is listed at $600 for the year. Breakout information should include the assumption that you will do three mailings for your annual appeal, membership, and annual meeting at $200 each, a figure that accounts for paper, printing, and postage. Numbers should be fully justified, and you may want to even talk to vendors or simply conduct research online as you compile your operating budget to ensure the practicality of your budget projections. Make sure you acknowledge all potential expenses, and be conservative to give yourself some wiggle room. Once you have accounted for all potential expenses, build your anticipated revenue sources, including earned and contributed sources. This is of particular importance in budget discussions with a board: it is the commitment to raising and earning funds to control the planned expenses for the year. Your budget should, of course, be balanced.

Your first operating budget will by necessity be a zero-based budget, meaning built from the ground up. Be careful of relying on past years' projections in future years and make sure that the operating budget reflects expansion or reduction when appropriate. If your site will be closed for six months to accommodate a restoration project, both your anticipated expenses and especially revenue projections should be scaled accordingly. Additionally, as your organization matures and you have multiple years of actuals, you will want to include one to three years of backup information to provide historical context for budget projects. See table 4.2 for a sample operating budget.

You may be asking: so what do I *do* with an operating budget, and how do I manage expenses to understand long-term implications of everyday activity? The best thing you can do is to implement a regular structure of processing payables, issuing reports, and checking in with board members. I recommend handing the processing of invoices daily or weekly, following determination of approvals structures between board and staff. That is, you will want to work out a system of approvals with the board; will the administrator be able to approve expenses up to a certain amount, perhaps $500? Will expenses above a certain threshold, perhaps $2,500, require executive committee or full board approval? The treasurer of the board is charged with financial oversight on behalf of the board, and she or he should coordinate with the administrator regarding a system of approvals; if no administrator is yet hired, determine a plan to outsource payables processing.

Table 4.2. Sample Operating Budget

	Operating Budget Template			
Fiscal Year	Current Budget	YTD Actuals	Previous FY Budget	Previous FY Budget	Over/Under Budget
Revenue					
Government Grants					
Foundation Support					
Corporate Support					
Individual Contributions					
Fundraising Events					
Membership and Program Income					
Other					
Total Cash Revenue					
Total In-kind Revenue					
Total Revenue					

Expenses			
Salaries and Wages			
Payroll Taxes			
Insurance			
Contracted Services			
Books and Supplies			
Purchases for Resale			
Travel			
Utilities			
Telecommunications			
Postage and Delivery			
Fundraising			
Postage and Delivery			
Total Cash Expenses			
Total In-Kind Expenses			
Total Expenses			
Revenue over Expenses			

The regular approval of invoices should consist not just of payment but also of classifying each expense according to the proper category (printing and publication, fees, shipping, etc.). This is where QuickBooks can be quite helpful in instituting the financial system. If you don't have access to software, simply create a coding system for your expenses and mark invoices when they are paid. This way, you will have a record of the payment processing and coding. Update your P&L monthly with any sources/uses of income, and the expenses paid. This should be shared at least with your board treasurer. On a monthly or a quarterly schedule, compare your P&L against your annual budget and make revisions to your forecast (your planned activity for the rest of the year) if necessary. Did your appeal mailing cost double what you anticipated? Analyzing your expenditures regularly against your budget figures is the lynchpin between daily, operational money needs and strategic financial management. When necessary, make narrative notes regarding adjustments or things to keep in mind regarding upcoming costs or sources of revenue. This information will form the basis for your audited financial statements.

Special Project Budgets

Your operating budget will be your "home base" budget and should be reflective of all operating activity. But what about when you want to raise money for and track expenses associated with a project such as a multiyear installation or a capital project? Such projects often span multiple fiscal years and can be tricky to manage if solely listed on the operating budget. Additionally, you may want to break out sources and uses of income for such a project, not just for tracking purposes but also for reporting to funders. In any case, project budgets document all costs associated with a particular project from start to finish, including all related expenses and all sources, and indirect expenses (such as staff time for project oversight) (see table 4.3). Expenses may be broken out according to fiscal year expenditures, which you may find helpful when correlating a project budget with your operating budget.

Table 4.3. Sample Project Budget: Exhibition

Revenue	Budget	Sources
Individuals	15,000	$15,000
Foundations and Corporations	15,000	$17,500
Institutional Funds	15,000	$10,150
Total Revenue	**45,000**	**$42,650**

Uses	Budget	Expenses
Organization		
Guest Curator	5,000	5000
Shipping	11,000	10500
Packing/Crating/Couriers	10,000	9075
Couriers	2,100	2175
Framing	3,500	3500
Conservation	1,500	1285
Extra Insurance	2,500	2500
Subtotal	**35,600**	**34,035**
Installation		
Custom Materials	500	350
Additional Security	250	0
Subtotal	**750**	**350**
Education		
Stipends/honoraria	500	450
Travel	750	700
Hospitality	500	650
Subtotal	**1,750**	**1,800**
Promotion		
Marketing/Advertising/Promotion	1,500	1235
Printed Materials	500	500
Displays and Banners	2,000	1945
Subtotal	**4,000**	**3,680**
Catalogue		
Publication	2,500	2385
Shipping	400	400
Subtotal	**2,900**	**2,785**
Total Expenses	**45,000**	**$42,650**
Total Surplus/Deficit		**0**

One particular type of project budget is a capital project budget, which can usually convey one of two things. First, a project budget, as detailed previously, bridges fiscal years and for which you wish to document all associated costs and income. The $750,000 capital project as described in the Bidwell Museum case study, for instance, requires a capital project budget. The other type of capital budget recognizes *all* the potential expenditures for building additions and improvements, beyond the parameters of a single capital project. Perhaps you wish to record all capital expenditures during a fiscal period for a report to a funder, or to establish a capital reserve fund, an account dedicated to long-term capital investment projects or anticipated expenses. In either case, capital activities often fall beyond the structure of the typical operating budget and should be well documented, especially in historic sites with ongoing capital activity, for alignment with annual audit.

* * *

Case Study: The Conrad Mansion Museum[8]
Kalispell, Montana

> Mission: To preserve and exhibit the 1895 Charles Conrad Family Estate through public tours, educational programs, and community events.[9]

Following the Civil War, Charles E. Conrad left his home in Virginia and moved west. Along with his brother William, he settled in Fort Benton, Montana, and established a shipping and freighting company that went on to serve as a major transportation hub in Montana. In 1891, he and his family moved to Flathead Valley, where he was one of the founders of Kalispell, Montana. Conrad aimed to build a home for his recently resettled family in Kalispell, but architects were hard to find on the frontier. He ultimately commissioned the Spokane, Washington–based architect Kirtland Cutter to construct a shingle-style home, which was finally completed in 1895. The house has been called a premier example of "luxurious pioneer living" by the National Trust for Historic Preservation; it has a rustic exterior and an interior in a Norman aesthetic, along with several technologically advanced amenities such as a freight elevator, a communications system, and built-in fire hoses.[10]

Conrad's daughter, Alicia Conrad Campbell, wished to save the contents of the house and preserve the site as a museum. She gave the property to the City of Kalispell in 1974, which initially refused the donation over concerns of the upkeep costs.[11] A deal was struck that the city would support the site for one year, and the mansion would be self-supporting in the future. The Conrad Mansion Museum was formally established by the end of 1974 and as agreed, has been owned by the city but fully financially independent since its first year of operation. In its first year, the recently established board of directors prioritized urgent repairs and cleaning, and the rehabilitation of the site moved from the first floor to the second and ultimately the third over the years. Between the items bequeathed by Campbell and original artifacts that have been returned to the site, the house has 95 percent of its original furnishings.

Today, the Conrad Mansion Museum has a budget of $180,000, receives approximately eight thousand visitors annually, and is operated by fifteen part-time staff members in season, and three part-time staff members in the off-season. Revenue is earned via tour admissions for individuals, groups, and off-season special tours, as well as gift shop sales, private event rentals, and fundraiser events. Individual donations and memberships, proceeds from the donation box, and board contributions comprise the majority of contributed income, with grant funding solicited for special projects such as capital repairs. While the museum earns income from investments, including an endowment, all investment income, including interest, is saved as reserve funding. The Conrad Mansion Museum budgets to cover operating expenses, which include utilities, payroll, and site maintenance, with earned and contributed income.

Executive Director Gennifer Sauter arrived in 2012 with a limited background in museums, but with strong business acumen learned through twenty years of experience as a financial manager and comptroller in the US Air Force. She manages activity daily using QuickBooks and issues a monthly P&L to the board of directors. These monthly statements provide the basis for budget revisions and regularize strategic funding discussions with the board. On a quarterly basis she works with an accounting firm, sharing QuickBooks reports from which information is culled to draft quarterly payroll tax reports. Sauter explains that the annual operating budget of $180,000 is stable and well informed, no doubt because of her practical approach to expenses: "The most important thing is to plan for expenses first. Once you know how much you need to put out, you know you much you need to bring in."[12]

What can we learn?

- Collaborative oversight and shared knowledge of financial activity make check-ins between staff and board members easier and more productive. The more conversant the members of an organization are in their numbers of an organization, the better they can prepare budgets and handle unforeseen needs.
- Build budgets from expenses and determine the funding you require, not the other way around.

Conclusion

Financial management is the process by which income and expenses are managed, documented, and reported. This chapter has provided an overview of the financial statements used for the annual audit as well as introductions to the fundamental methods of accounting, including budget planning. As you initiate financial activity at your site, you will want to consider the following means by which to monitor financial activity.

Key Points: Checklist

- Planning for Financial Tracking and Oversight
  - Confirm Professional Relationships with Accounting Firm (and Potentially a Bookkeeper)
  - Formalize Approvals Structure
  - Obtain Financial Management Software
  - Confirm Cash vs. Accrual Method
- Initiation of Financial Tracking
  - Review Business and Strategic Plans

- Determine Potential Revenue Sources and Expenses
- Draft Operating Budget
- Review of Financial Activity
  - Weekly Payables Processing
  - Monthly P&L Review and Comparison to Budget
  - Quarterly Review and Budget Adjustments with Board
  - Annual Operating Budget Preparation and Approval
- Annual Reporting of Financial Activity
  - Statement of Financial Activity
  - Statement of Financial Position
  - Statement of Cash Flows

Notes

1. Financial Accounting Standards Board, "Financial Statements of Not-for-profit Organizations (Issued 6/93)," http://www.fasb.org/summary/stsum117.shtml.

2. Patricia Egan and Nancy Sasser, "Understanding Financial Statements," in *The Art of Governance—Boards in the Performing Arts*, eds. Nancy Roche and Jaan Whitehead (New York: Theatre Communications Group, 2005).

3. Depreciation, or the reduction in value of an asset over time, is worth a side note to discuss as it relates to historic sites. While buildings and moveable assets—among other things—are considered a capital asset and capitalized (or depreciated) over time for the purposes of financial reporting, you do not want to assume such for historic buildings or your collections. Though they age, many—if not most—historical sites do not want to monetize their collections (aside from for insurance purposes) because they are not considered assets available for use that, in worst cases, means liquidization. Depreciation and capitalization rates are determined at the state level, and many states recognize the exception of historical treasures and works of art from these rates. A good rule of thumb is that if your site has capitalized these objects in the past, continue to do so to avoid disruption in your reporting. Otherwise, do not depreciate structures or objects of historical and/or artistic value.

4. While nonprofit organizations are indeed tax exempt, some of their expenses incorporate taxable activity. The most common example is taxes paid on wages.

5. Interview with Barbara Palmer, Executive Director.

6. http://bidwellhousemuseum.org/index.php/about-us/.

7. Barbara Palmer, personal communication, February 7, 2017.

8. Interview with Gennifer Sauter, Executive Director.

9. http://www.conradmansion.com/About-Museum.html.

10. National Trust for Historic Preservation, "Distinctive Destinations: Conrad Mansion Museum," savingplaces.org/places/Conrad-mansion-museum #.WJ3rARIrJTY.

11. Katrin Frye, "Why Kalispell First Said 'No' to Owning the Historic Conrad Mansion," *MTPR Morning Edition and Montana News*, Montana Public Radio, February 11, 2014.

12. Gennifer Sauter, personal communication, February 7, 2017.

5

Blueprints for the Future

Financial Forecasting and Strategic Planning

Before we get started on our last chapter (we're in the home stretch, readers!), let's pause and check in. Our first chapters were probably well within your wheelhouse and to be expected: mission, contributions, and earned revenue. You may have had previous experience with these topics and arrived in your current situation—whether as a board member, administrator, or volunteer—with some degree of knowledge that you are in the process of perfecting. In the previous chapter, we delved into the specific work of financial management; in this chapter we will provide further insights into the using that information to build reports, forecast future activity, and provide information to the Internal Revenue Service via the Form 990.

For many individuals in historic house museums and other sites, this topic may be well out of your comfort zone. Just remember that you are sharing your story and activity using the language of numbers. Many, if not most, nonprofit professionals consider the annual reporting cycle—and specifically completion of Form 990—to be a stressful and time-consuming exercise that tests their patience and knowledge. And sure, you could have that completely valid opinion—I get it. Or, you could seize the opportunity provided in such an activity to better understand your work over the year, explore your organizational strengths and challenges, and arm yourself for the future to best achieve your mission.

Financial Reporting and Planning

The concept of financial reporting can take a number of forms. We have addressed the need for a reporting structure between staff and board, which should be formalized and documented. Reporting should be addressed according to a predetermined arrangement, and it should never be done informally. Reports of spending and income-generating activities should be generated and reviewed, at least at the staff level, and at least monthly. Internal reporting from a staff member to a board—or from a finance committee to the board—should be handled at least quarterly. Preparation in advance is acceptable and advisable. Reporting information should be shared in official board meetings and entered into the minutes. I recommend creating a document that encompasses all financial activity during a particular period, at least quarterly, that provides a comparison to budget figures and past year actuals, if available. The sample quarterly report in table 5.1 compares annual operating figures to actuals to-date, previous year actual data, and a forecasting column.

Financial Forecasting

This brings us to a key point, that of forecasting.[1] Some of us may have little experience with financial forecasting, and only hear the word "forecasting" in reference to weather reports. But a forecast, which is literally a prediction or an estimate, is an imperative financial process. Similar to budget building, forecasting is the exercise in which you predict the activity to take place in the remainder of a fiscal period (usually a year), or in relation to a specific project, and document revised estimates. If you compile reports on a quarterly basis, this information will be most useful in your second and third quarters for the simple reason that your first quarter will most likely provide little deviation from the original budget, and your last quarter will result in final, actual

Table 5.1. Sample Quarterly Report.

	Budget 2016/17	YTD Actuals (Q2)	Forecast 2016/17	Actuals 2015/16
SAMPLE QUARTERLY REPORT				
Income				(YTD)
Endowment Distribution	3,750	1,746	4,075	3,500
Total—endowment	*3,750*	*1,746*	*4,075*	*3,500*
Contributed Funds				
Federal and State Funding	75,000	26,750	55,000	70,250
Corporate and Foundation Grants	100,000	37,500	78,000	75,650
Memberships	25,000	21,025	42,000	23,210
Individual Gifts	25,000	18,200	30,000	24,662
Other Contributions	3,000	1,680	3,000	3,820
Total—contributed funds	*228,000*	*105,155*	*208,000*	*197,592*
Earned Income				
Admissions	12,500	7,513	16,000	12,486
Gift shop sales	25,000	15,087	32,000	28,075
Other income	5,750	4,233	8,500	6,172
Total—earned income	*43,250*	*26,833*	*56,500*	*46,733*
Total income	**275,000**	**133,734**	**268,575**	**247,825**
Expenses				
Payroll				
Wages and Salaries	49,000	24,038	48,075	46,152
Health and other benefits	16,500	8,004	16,500	15,369
Subtotal—payroll	*65,500*	*32,042*	*64,575*	*61,521*
Programs				
Exhibitions	27,500	14,565	25,000	18,838
School Groups	3,400	2,426	4,000	2,841
Specialized Tours and Education	3,000	600	2,250	773
Subtotal—programs	*33,900*	*17,591*	*31,250*	*22,451*
General Administration				
Contracted services	6,000	3,524	5,000	5,824
Supplies/Other	16,500	13,026	17,500	15,512
Printing and Publication	5,000	2,527	5,000	4,450
Travel	1,000	203	500	490
Campaign Events	4,000	1,628	4,000	3,838
Gift shop purchases	17,500	9,499	18,750	16,795
Subtotal—administration	*50,000*	*30,407*	*50,750*	*46,908*
Facilities				
Maintenance	25,000	10,035	25,000	23,060
Utilities	62,000	30,063	61,500	59,523
Insurance	26,000	13,000	26,000	25,000
Equipment, technology	2,600	117	2,000	1,473
Subtotal—facilities	*115,600*	*53,215*	*114,500*	*109,056*
Acquisitions	10,000	480	7,500	7,890
Subtotal—acquisitions	*10,000*	*480*	*7,500*	*7,890*
Total expenses	**275,000**	**133,734**	**268,575**	**247,825**
Surplus / (Deficit)	—	—	—	—

numbers. But in the third and fourth quarters, forecasting creates a bridge between the financial record of actual activity on a day-to-day basis and your budget. And while there is often the opportunity to update project budgets as a capital project or an exhibition evolves, operating budgets are not updated once approved: to create a financial forecast is to review the income versus expenses, and essentially move the puzzle pieces as needed. Did you shoot for the moon with a grant application and just receive word that you got it, which allows you to plan to grow a project? Your forecast reflects the anticipated income and the growth in expenses. Can you tell in January that you will fall short of your membership goal by roughly 20 percent? Document the revised income in your forecast, as well as where you will cut back your expenses to accommodate the shortfall.

The creation of a forecast is, like a budget, reliant upon your best guesses. The knowledge shared by board members and staff members inform such an exercise, as do cost estimates (such as the cost of a new piece of equipment) and costs that are stable throughout the year (such as a flat rate heating or insurance payment plan). As your organization matures, historical data from past years will be increasingly valuable in the annual budget process and will help you understand the rhythm of activity throughout the year. To regularly revise a forecast is to create the foundation for sound financial management throughout the fiscal year, actively engaging both operating expectations and the real data of current activity. That is what we want to avoid: to end up at the conclusion of a year wildly over budget and panicked over the financial situation as you look to the future. This is proper management: to monitor your finances on a regular basis and work proactively *and* reactively, even if you fall short of a fundraising goal or have to spend extra on a burst pipe in the basement.

Along with your forecasting, which is likely on a quarterly basis, I recommend taking a similar approach to your fundraising plan. While you may not be able to predict your contributions with real accuracy, you can utilize the quarterly approach to coordinate and streamline fundraising efforts. Utilizing the actual data and forecast revisions, consider in terms of fundraising and how to prioritize fundraising goals. That burst pipe in the basement may be an expense that depletes your institutional coffers, ultimately leaving fewer funds available for programming. Armed with this knowledge, plan for and document how you plan to fund such a project using funds in-hand plus money you will raise. Coordinating forecasting and strategic fundraising planning creates an internal workflow that recognizes the interdependency of the money you bring in and the management of funds. See figure 5.1 for a sample fundraising chart.

Reporting to External Agencies and Donors

Reporting to external organizations and to the general public is a bit different. As we know, funding agencies often call the shots in terms of how, when, and in what form they wish to receive a report. Always adhere to the specifications agencies offer, which explain the parameters required for stewardship reports—divergence from stated agency policies could be the difference between receiving future funding and not. Project-specific funding from individuals should also be handled according to a relevant schedule and in addition to the acknowledgment for tax purposes. For a capital project, perhaps send donors an update at benchmark moments in the project trajectory, such as the completion of the first phase of a three-phase restoration project, or when a major matching gift has been attained and contributions must be solicited to match the gift. Reporting to donors should be preplanned for two reasons, both to do with pacing and information: to reach out too often is to inundate people with information they do not necessarily want and potentially cause them to tune out any correspondence from you or your organization; to reach out not often enough is to alienate donors from your progress, and people could feel that their investment in your work is not valued. A successful model is to create a regular structure of providing updates directly to your donor base regarding specific projects for which you solicited funding, and if you have additional information to share, do so on a public platform, such as on your website or in your newsletter.

Figure 5.1. Fundraising Chart.

Sample Planning Document: Funding
Funding Worksheet: Upcoming Projects

	Project Budget	Institutional Funds	Funds Raised	Fundraising Goal (Amount to Fund)
Project One	5,000	2,000	2,500	500
Project Two	2,500	-	1,000	1,500
Project Three	28,500	5,000	-	23,500
Project Four	10,000	4,400	5,000	600
Total:	46,000	11,400	8,500	26,100

Potential Funder (Nan	Project One	Project Two	Project Three	Project Four	Ask Amount	Workflow Status	General Notes
AAA Foundation	2,500				5,000	Stewardship	50% funded; report letter due 1 year from project opening
BBB Corporation		1,000			1,000	Awarded	Notification letter received; awaiting payment
Mr. and Mrs. John Jones			-		10,000	Rejected	No funding available in FY17; approach in FY18
Mr. and Mrs. Bob Smith				5,000	5,000	Pledged	Contributions to be received monthly January-October FY17

The Annual Report

In addition to the structured reporting regarding special projects or to agencies, many organizations compile an annual report. A published annual report is not required by the government, but is a useful document for its comprehensive overview of the year's activities. It often includes the financial documents of the statement of financial activity, statement of financial position, and cash flow statement and should align with the information submitted to the IRS in the Form 990. Narrative components of the annual report typically address major projects that took place throughout the year, perhaps acquisitions if your organization holds a permanent collection, progress on capital restoration or expansion if relevant, and achievement of strategic goals, such as education and public engagement. Financial information can be distilled into informative pie charts or graphs, and photographs showcase events, tours, and other programming. Most annual reports document support in a list of contributors.

While not required, the issuance of an annual report is often a good idea. First, it provides an easy reference of annual activity. This can be useful for internal reference purposes, and to serve as a sort of "yearbook" of programs, projects, and finances. Second, the annual report can serve as a worthwhile promotional tool to offer prospective donors, members, and other community members. If and when you are in the position to solicit funds or to promote the organization, an annual report can serve as a key document to introduce a variety of audiences and potential stakeholders to your site and the kind of work that you do. An annual report can be informative and can get people excited about your site and its mission. Does this sound like a great idea, but one that is difficult to imagine on your current budget? Consider designing an annual report for your website and online distribution to your email list, or a narrative report with a few pictures to highlight achievements. Financial information is useful but not compulsory, and such a document is a great way to broadcast your work.

* * *

Case Study: The Neill-Cochran House Museum[2]
Austin, Texas

Mission: To promote the national and state heritage through historic preservation of the Neill-Cochran House Museum (Austin, Texas), patriotic service, and educational projects. The organization is affiliated with the National Society of the Colonial Dames of America.[3]

The Neill-Cochran House was constructed directly following the establishment of Austin as the capital of Texas in 1855, during a period of rapid expansion in the central Texas region. Local builder and designer Abner Cook was commissioned to construct a Greek Revival structure on eighteen acres of land just northwest of the city limits for land surveyor Washington Hill. Hill ran out of funding before the house was completed and never actually resided on the property, which was purchased by local investors S. M. Swenson and John Milton Swisher, who leased the house to a number of tenants over the next two decades. The property remained a residence after its sale to C. W. Whitis and then to Scottish immigrant and lawyer Andrew Neill and his family. In 1895, lawyer and recently appointed circuit court judge Thomas Cochran and his wife Bessie purchased the home, which remained in the Cochran family until 1958. That year, the property was sold to the National Society of Colonial Dames in the State of Texas, who initiated preservation efforts and turned the site into a museum in 1962.

Since 1958, the National Society of Colonial Dames in the State of Texas has overseen the preservation, maintenance, and programming of the site, which consists of the house, the eighteen-acre property, and a stone dependency, believed to be the only still-standing slave quarters in central Texas.[4] The funding situation is one common among historic house museums, in which a parent organization provides major funding; in this case, the Colonial Dames provide roughly 90 percent of the funding of the Neill-Cochran House, which essentially functions as a department of the larger organization as its headquarters. Executive Director Rowena Dasch explains that the Neill-Cochran House Museum reports through the state board of the

Colonial Dames, which has a formal committee dedicated to the affairs of the museum. The committee functions as an "ally" of the museum and promotes the interests and financial needs of the museum to the larger board responsible for all affairs of the Colonial Dames. The approximately $200,000/year budget of the mansion is created and maintained by Dasch, along with the treasurer of the Colonial Dames state board in her capacity representing the finance committee of the board. Dasch and the state treasurer meet regularly and Dasch reports to the museum committee three times per year.

Earned income is earned through tours, workshops, special programs, and event rentals, and contributed income is brought in through voluntary contributions via membership and other campaigns. Additional income is generated from investment distributions. Transactions are managed via Square software, which also monitors attendance, admissions, and rental activity. This activity, along with gift processing, is managed using QuickBooks. The museum also makes use of a checking account and a credit card for expenses. Monthly activity reports are produced from QuickBooks, which serve as the basis for the three annual meetings with the Neill-Cochran House Museum Committee.

Dasch explains that though the relationship with the Colonial Dames is well structured, she faces a challenge common among parent-stewarded organizations, that of funding allocation. While the museum generated income, much of that earned and contributed revenue supports the state organization, and money brought in via house activities go to the state to be redistributed back to the museum. Dasch looks to create additional funding streams, particularly through corporate and foundation grants restricted to museum use. While the museum has realized success with regional and state agencies so far, Dasch comments that a strategic goal of hers is to build community engagement via structured giving in order to encourage direct funding of the museum. The Neill-Cochran House Museum illuminates a house museum in transition, in which Dasch recognizes the need to encourage self-sustainability while managing a fruitful relationship with a parent organization.

What can we learn?

- Never forget the need to diversify support streams. While the museum received regular support from the Colonial Dames, Dasch still priorities the need to gain traction with her community to promote future museum interests.
- Museum-steward relationships can be difficult to negotiate, especially in consideration of mutually exclusive priorities. Make your site a priority and be sure to structure and document all communication between your site and parent organization to ensure a smooth relationship.

* * *

The Form 990

We've talked about some ways to approach your finances throughout the year to ensure practical and productive use of your financial information, and you may already be visualizing your annual report of the future, a glossy brochure with a long list of donors and photos that show children playing on the lawn in front of a restored veranda, or a beautiful spring day in which people are crowded into the house to view your newest exhibition. And that may very well be in your future! But before we get there, we have to tackle the last and most vital step in the financial management of your site since the date of incorporation: the filing of the Form 990, formally known as the "Return of Organization Exempt from Income Tax," with the Internal Revenue Service.

Two caveats before we fully turn our attention to the 990. First, this is not the only annual reporting requirement. Each state has its own reporting requirements and may even require an external audit above a certain income, and the relevant state office for your organization should be consulted to ensure you are correctly addressing reporting to the state. Second, I will provide a detailed reading of the 990 based on typical and general information. There are endless unique situations particular to each organization that require specific attention, understanding, and documentation. My word is not the final word on any of the following, and should only be used for general reference.

Form 990 does not have a great reputation, I will admit. The regulations change regularly, the directions can be hard to understand for those new to the field, and many in nonprofits grumble that it is a challenge to complete the 990 and it is an exercise that saps staff time or funds to work with an accountant. But personally, I love 990s. I read 990s for fun. *For fun!* Why would I subject myself to such torture? Because the 990 is a fantastic resource to learn about organizations in our field. Invaluable information regarding board membership, salaries and wages, membership activity, grant activity, programming and associated costs—you name it, you can discover it through an organization's Form 990. I say this not voyeuristically, but in the sense that you can most fully comprehend what is happening in the field through reviews of 990s. Especially if you are new to nonprofits in your service as a board or a staff member, 990s are the most informative resource to use in preparation of your organization's filing, or to simply look at what other organizations are doing. Since the financial information of all 501(c)(3) organizations is open and available to the public, websites have made such information available for public viewing. Charitynavigator.org and guidestar.org are two sites that are useful resources for 990s (check subscription requirements). To be sure, there is a flip side to this equation: do not forget that the public transparency and availability of 990s apply to your site as well. For all obvious reasons related to the IRS and also to their accessibility, you want to ensure your information is accurate.

When should you complete a Form 990? You must report your activity to the IRS on an annual basis. The 990 is due to the IRS on a schedule of four and a half months after the close of your fiscal year. If your organization functions on a fiscal year that begins July 1 and ends June 30, your 990 is due on November 15. If you run on a calendar year, the 990 for the year ending December 31 is due on May 15. Whatever the case, make a note to compile your supporting documents well in advance of the deadline. Extensions are available by filing the Form 8868:

Application for Extension of Time to File an Exempt Organization Return, and are commonly granted. Do not, under any circumstances, miss filing deadlines without petitioning for an extension. Penalties are severe for late submissions and an unnecessary expense that no nonprofit needs. Plus, you want to do everything in your power to stay in the good graces of the IRS.

Dependent on your gross receipts, which comprise all income from all sources before expenses are subtracted, you will be required to file one of the following forms: 990-N, 990EZ, or 990. A 990-N Electronic Notice is required for those organizations whose gross receipts total less than $25,000 and consists of a very simple form to be completed online. This may be the case for your organization in its earliest years of operation. The 990EZ is for organizations that bring in $200,000 or less in a year *and* hold assets valued at less than $500,000. The valuation of your assets should be on your balance sheet for reference. If your organization receives $200,000 or more in a year, *or* has more than $500,000 in assets, that organization must file the full 990. You want to keep an eye on your organizational finances, as well as any potential IRS updates to this structure, to be sure you are filing the paperwork that corresponds to your gross receipts and assets. Let's now look at the individual parts of the 990 to gain a complete overview of the process.

Introductory Information

Form 990 begins with the request for introductory information; this information should reflect the incorporation documents formalized in chapter 1 of this book. Boxes are included for the organization name, principal officer (defined by the IRS as "a person who, regardless of title, has ultimate responsibility for implementing the decisions of the organization's governing body, or for supervising the management, administration, and operation of the organization").[5] Here you include the dates of your tax year, date and state of incorporation, and declare your tax exemption status along with the employer identification number.

Also in the introductory section is a box for you to include the figure for gross receipts, which is the income the organization has received from all sources before the subtraction of expenses. This information is included in the introductory section to ensure that the organization is filing the appropriate form that aligns with their size.

Part I: Summary

Part I is essentially a summary of the information offered in the rest of the 990, divided into four sections. Lines 1 through 7b provide space to detail the activities and governance of the organization, including mission, board members, staff, and volunteers, all of which provide organizational size context to the numbers to follow. In this section you have the opportunity to declare UBIT, all income unrelated to the mission.

The remaining sections summarize information delineated in following sections of the form, and should be completed after the corresponding parts of the 990 have been completed. The revenue section (lines 8 through 12) report how much total income the filer received in the reporting period, including contributions and grants, program services, investment income, and other revenue. All of this information is generated in Part VIII, Statement of Revenue. Completing Part VIII first is advisable, and then those totals can simply be incorporated into Part I. Similarly, the expenses section (lines 13 through 19) provides a review of all expenses, including grants and contributions paid, member benefits, salaries, compensation, and other benefits, fundraising fees and expenses, and other expenses, which are culled from Part IX, the Statement of Functional Expenses. Line 19, revenue less expenses, is the net income of the organization. This comparison of revenue to expenses is an indicator of the health of the organization.[6]

The final section, dedicated to net assets or fund balances (lines 20 through 22), includes information derived from Part X, the Balance Sheet. Completion of Parts VIII, IX, and X will ensure consistency between the different parts of the 990.

Part II: Signature Block

The signature block is the declaration that all information provided in the 990 is accurate to the best knowledge of both an officer of the organization, usually the board president or treasurer, as well as a paid preparer. I strongly recommend utilizing the services of an accountant for every 990 preparation but especially in your first year, to ensure you are properly reporting your activity.

Part III: Statement of Program Service Accomplishments

The Statement of Program Service Accomplishments is extremely important, for it is in this past that you justify your tax-exempt status with information about the program services you offer. After providing your mission (line 1), you are asked three questions about changes to your program services and activities since the previous year's filing. If you do have major changes to report, this information is entered in Schedule O. In your first year filing, you will not have a previous year 990 for reference, and an introduction to your services in Part III, lines 4a–4c should suffice.

Lines 4a–4c are dedicated to the program service accomplishments of the organization's three largest areas of service. Note that size is determined by expense, so these are the three mission-based activities on which the most money is spent. You are asked to provide accomplishments, which are understood by way of measurable data of people served. What are your attendance figures? How many students participated in educational programming, and how many different programs were offered during the reporting period? Quantitative evidence of services offered and people reached are most useful here, though supplemental information can be included in Schedule O if necessary.

In addition to listing the top three program services and related accomplishments, also include the expenses and revenue for each program. The 990 includes an option to list a grant figure in your expenses, which is most likely not applicable to your organization. Keep in mind that many tax-exempt organizations disseminate funds; in this case, the grant information is in regard to grants given, not grants received.

Line 4d allows for the inclusion of any other program services not accommodated in lines 4a–4c, which are to be described in Schedule O. Line 4e equals the total of program service expenses from all lines in Part III. This number will be listed again in Part IX, the Statement of Functional Expenses, in column B of line 25. Your total program service expense is reflective of the proportion of spending on programs versus other expenses, particularly related to management or fundraising (or both). The higher the proportion of funding of programs versus other activities proves the primacy of program services to your organization and is a useful demonstration of tax-exempt status.

Part IV: Checklist of Required Schedules

Tax schedules are forms the IRS requires in relation to specific activities, often to income-generating programs. The current checklist consists of thirty-eight questions, some with subquestions that require a "yes" or "no" answer. Depending on your response to each question, you may be directed to complete additional schedules or portions of schedules. Your answers to these questions are particular to your organization's activity over the year, and provide information that enables the IRS to determine compliance with 501(c)(3) regulations.

Part V: Statements Regarding Other IRS Filings and Tax Compliance

Similar to the Checklist of Required Schedules, the Statements Regarding Other IRS Filings and Tax Compliance is a checklist of other forms that may be required, which depends on your activity, and is designed to ensure compliance with tax codes and tax-exempt status. Many of the questions reference proper procedures, such as the documentation of contributions with

acknowledgments provided to donors, or the correct categoriza-
tion of personnel into employees and independent contractors.
Unlike Part IV, the questions in Part V do not lead the filer to
additional schedules for completion, but the answers question
the measures taken to document financial and legal activity. If
explanations of your answers would be helpful, those are not
required but can be included in Schedule O.

Part VI: Governance, Management, and Disclosure

The questions in Part VI offer an opportunity in three sections
to detail the structure of your organization, including its leadership, policies, and public transparency. Part VI, Section A: Governing Body and Management is the portion of the 990 in which
you describe the board leadership and constituency, meeting
and policy documentation, and the formalization of your
bylaws. Review of Section A is worthwhile outside of 990 completion, especially when reviewing or revising your bylaws.
Make sure your bylaws address all topics addressed herein so
that your internal documents parallel the information you report
to the IRS. Section B: Policies, for example, provides an opportunity to review the procedures of the organization in terms of
reporting activity to donors. Though the IRS comments that this
section "requests information about policies not required by the
Internal Revenue Code," it is best to treat this section like any
other required in the 990.[7] All information you can offer that
provides evidence of consistent documentation and strong oversight of your organization is most important. Any answers that
illustrate a change in oversight (such as revisions to the bylaws)
may raise questions, so always describe any changes in this section in the Schedule O.

Part C: Disclosure is quite straightforward. You are required
to file the 990 in each state in which the organization does business, which is usually limited to your state of incorporation. You
should not, however, make any assumptions, and I encourage
you to visit this question with a tax professional each year and
as your activity grows. This disclosure statement also addresses

the means by which you make your tax documents available for public inspection, as well as to name the individual responsible for the organizational books and records. This information is required to guarantee that the financial information is available to the public, which is stipulated of all nonprofit organizations in the United States.

Part VII: Compensation of Officers, Directors, Trustees, Key Employees, Highest Compensated Employees, and Independent Contractors

Part VII delineates the compensation and benefits paid to board members or staff members. Most nonprofit organizations do not compensate their board members, though some are paid for their time or expertise in certain cases. Should any payment be allocated to a board member, be sure to document it here.

In terms of staff compensation, the IRS is interested in comparing staff compensation in the context of their responsibilities and organizational size. "Key Employee" is a term instituted by the IRS to delineate those that earn above a certain financial threshold (which changes regularly and in accordance with cost-of-living changes) and hold decision-making power. The salaries and benefits of key employees are reviewed to make sure their compensation is fair given the current and comparable nonprofit market and in relation to the funding allocated to program activities, which should be the top priority for charitable organizations.

The roster of board members and staff members is the government record of the leadership of your organization, and speaks to its quality and structure. How diverse is the board: Are multiple members from one family? Are there too few or too many board members? Independent board members, those without a material or pecuniary relationship to the organization, should typically comprise your board for optimal strength and diversity of perspectives.

Part VII, Section B documents compensation to independent contractors who are paid more than $100,000 in a year.[8] Many organizations will not exceed $100,000 in contractor agreements in a given year—and Section B would thus be left blank—but that may indeed occur in a year of a major capital project or as an organization grows. In any case, the reporting of compensation to contractors is an easily misunderstood section. You want to keep in mind that whenever an independent contractor provides services (not merchandise or goods), you will file a Form 1099-MISC with the IRS, though the reportable activity is by no means limited to those contractors for whom a 1099-MISC is completed. Fees to a brokerage firm for investment management or rent paid would also be included in the section, for instance.

Part VIII: Statement of Revenue

The Statement of Revenue includes documentation of all sources of income in the year. The data provided by an organization indicates how it is run and the diversity of its funding sources. Is there a balance between contributed and earned income? Are the non-mission–related activities to which UBIT applies too high, which thus jeopardizes the tax exemption? Such questions can be answered in Part VIII, which should parallel the information provided in the organization's statement of financial activity (see chapter 4).

The Statement of Revenue, divided into three sections, documents in lines 1a–1h all contributions, gifts, grants, and all other gifted funds. The second section, lines 2a–2g, account for all program service revenue. Your program service revenue should correlate with the revenue listed in Part III, the Statement of Program Service Accomplishments. Other Revenue, lines 3–10c, is where other revenue such as that garnered from fundraising events, rental income, or sales of assets is recorded. If you have revenue-generating activity that does not quite fall into these three categories, lines 11a–11e offer space to enter miscellaneous revenue. The information entered in Part VIII is used to populate lines 8–12 in Part I of the 990.

Part IX: Statement of Functional Expenses

The Statement of Functional Expenses details the spending activity of the filer, sectioned into twenty-five questions that help the IRS understand how much the organization is spending on program services, its exempt purpose as a charitable organization, in relation to other activities. The first questions, lines 1–3, are in regard to grants made by the organization. Remember, these are not grants of which you are a beneficiary but instead are grants your organization awards. Lines 4–9 detail compensation to members, officers, and salaries, as well as benefits paid. The costs to manage compensation are listed in lines 10–11g, including payroll taxes and fees for services regarding management and other oversight. If any of these figures exceed $100,000, they should correspond with Part VII, Section B. General management and operation costs are articulated in lines 12–24e, and line 25 is the sum of the previous lines.

Note that expenses are further categorized into program service expenses (column B), management and general expenses (column C), and fundraising expenses (column D), with column A as their sum. In some cases, line item expenses will be segregated into all three expense categories, in some cases only one or two will be utilized. If you face confusion about which column to categorize expenses, keep in mind that column B is for program services, and thus only mission-related activities should be recorded in column B, the sum of which should correspond with the total expenses listed in Part III, Statement of Program Service Accomplishments, line 4e.

The fundraising category (column D) may seem extraneous at first, but it can often prove to be a significant expense for many organizations, sometimes overshadowing programming. Line 25d provides the cumulative amount dedicated to fundraising expenses. If you divide this line by 25a, you will arrive at the fundraising ratio, which documents the amount of money spent on fundraising versus total expenses. Useful for sophisticated donors to understand where their money is going, this can also help you to understand the relationship between the different expense categories.

The Statement of Functional Expenses and the corresponding section of Part I on the first page of the 990 are actually useful tools to measure the size of an organization. While large gifts intended to fund multiyear projects can skew the revenue side of your 990, the expenses encapsulate the activity of an organization most accurately. Consider this when managing your own 990, but also when reviewing the activity of other organizations in the field.

Part X: Balance Sheet

Along with Parts XIII and IX, Part X captures the heart of the activity of an organization in the fiscal year. To capture this information should not be an exercise that takes you by surprise, for it documents the same data collected annually in the major financial reports described in chapter 4. Together, these reports comprise all financial activity for the year and indicate overall organizational stability.

Like the organizational balance sheet described in the previous chapter, Part X lists assets, liabilities, and net assets or fund balances. Assets (lines 1–16) are listed in decreasing order of their liquidity, or availability for use in the near term. Conversely, liabilities (lines 17–26) are in decreasing necessity of payment. The lower the amount of liabilities the better, especially regarding payables that will affect immediate activity in the next fiscal year. Net assets are declared in lines 27–34, and relate the liabilities to the assets: if the liabilities exceed the assets and result in fund balances, the organization is in poor financial health. What else indicates financial health? Line 27, column b shows the unrestricted net assets available at the end of the year for future use. Along with reasonable and sustainable revenue, planning can ensure that expenses will be met in the future. Also worth mentioning is the difference between lines 28 and 29: line 28 documents temporarily restricted assets, which is for the short term, such as grant funding for a project that spans fiscal years; line 29 illustrates permanently restricted assets, such as endowment funds.

Part XI: Reconciliation of New Assets

Like Part I, Part XI is reliant upon the information entered in Part VIII, Part IX, and Part X, and thus those sections should be completed first. The information regarding revenue, expenses, and balances are listed herein. Note that line 10 should equal line 33, column B of Part X, which is the net assets or fund balances at the end of the year.

Part XII: Financial Statements and Reporting

Part XII captures any other relevant information, including the accounting method used to complete the 990 and how the 990 was compiled in relation to the other annual financial statements. Together, the completion of the 990 and the organizational completion and board approval of the financial documents comprise the audit process.

The Form 990 and the Planning Process

Once you have signed off on your Form 990, you are done with your annual duties, right? Perhaps, in terms of the legal requirement to file with the IRS, but otherwise there is still work to be done. Now that you have a complete Form 990, you have a document that essentializes your mission in terms of financial activity and allows you to view through an objective lens all of your work. Does your mission receive primacy in terms of funding? Where are you spending too much money (or too little)? How productive is your spending on fundraising activities? Should you revise your fundraising plan and perhaps hire—or release—a fundraising professional?

The standardization of Form 990 makes it a useful benchmark for organizational comparison within the nonprofit sector, and even more specifically among cultural organizations such as museums and historic sites. Do not forget the utility review of Form 990 can serve your board and staff as you incorporate and look to understand the professional landscape, but this information will also inform others about your work. Do your activities and funding allocations reflect a well-run organization? Is your spending proportionate to income and programmatic needs? Is your mission well articulated? Prospective donors and collaborators in the field may review your 990 to determine your financial health, so keep that in mind.

The Form 990 is also of use for internal planning purposes. As noted earlier in this chapter, the preparation period for the completion of your 990 is an apt time to review fundraising strategy and plan for the following year's priorities. Other activities, such as projects, can also be reviewed in accordance with the knowledge of the financial position documented in the 990. Consider creating a structure for receiving project proposals at a certain time of year and in correlation to the annual operating budget or 990 preparation cycles to best attend to funding needs and priorities (see figure 5.2).

* * *

Case Study: The Pittock Mansion[9]
Portland, Oregon

Mission: To inspire understanding and stewardship of Portland history through the Pittock Mansion, its collections, and programs.

By 1909, Portland, Oregon, had become a bustling commercial center due to the booming logging and distribution industries; it had also become a major port city on the West Coast. The owner and publisher of *The Oregonian* newspaper, Henry Pittock, and his wife, Georgiana, commissioned a palatial home that was built on the outskirts of the city. The house was constructed in the French Renaissance style and was completed in 1914. The Pittock family resided in the house for generations, and was eventually put up for sale in 1958. The house remained unoccupied for years and suffered major structural damage, most notably from a 1962 storm that damaged the roof and left the house interior exposed for eighteen months. Though developers attempted to purchase the property for reconfiguration as a subdivision, a citizens' grassroots campaign formed to save the structure and in 1964, the City of Portland intervened. The City of Portland purchased the property, utilizing over $67,000 raised from the community. Following fifteen months of repairs, the house was opened to the public as the Pittock Mansion in 1965.

Today, the Pittock Mansion is open from February through December and consists of the main house and a gate lodge, both interpreted spaces; a garage, which includes visitor services, the mansion store and ticketing; and administrative spaces. The mansion maintains a collection of art objects and decorative arts, many of them original, and a strategic priority of the mansion is to grow the collection of objects original to the residence of the Pittock family.

While still owned by the City of Portland, the Pittock Mansion underwent an organizational shift in 2007, precipitated jointly by the mansion board and the city. A management agreement was formalized that ensured the city would be accountable for the grounds, structures, and systems of the site, but would no longer provide the mansion with direct financial support. Since 2007, all costs of managing the mansion organization and interpretation of the site have been the responsibility of the Pittock Mansion Society and its board of directors. The current director, Marta Bones, arrived in 2007 in the midst of this transition with a background in nonprofit administration, though she had no experience in financial management.[10] The board of directors funded Bones's training in QuickBooks and basic accounting, as they recognized the need for autonomous financial oversight following the dissolution of the financial relationship with the City of Portland.

The finances of the Pittock Mansion are managed on monthly, quarterly, and annual cycles. All transactions, including the point-of-sale system, are integrated in with QuickBooks, and contributions are managed in Donor Perfect. Account reconciliations and transactional reviews are handled monthly; if the activity levels deviate substantially from projected budget figures, Bones speaks with the staff members responsible for departmental budgets. These monthly reports also include information on attendance as well as financial activity, and all data is compared to month-to-month and year-to-year historical information. The quarterly reports provide all of this information as well as fundraising updates and forecasting projections, all

Figure 5.2.   Project Proposal Form.

Primary Contact/Project Director:

Type of Project:

 o Capital Project   o Programming/Event o Exhibition

Partnering Institutions (if any):

Project Title:

Project Dates and Location.

Brief Description of Project: (Why do this project? Why now? How does it relate to mission?)

Other Considerations:

Proposed Project Elements:

Exhibition:

___ Loans Only	___ Permanent Collection w/ Loans	___ Outside Curator
___ Packaged Exhibition		___ Permanent
Collection Only		___ Traveling

 Collections and loans:

___ Conservation	___ Record Photography	___ Matting/Framing
___ Loan Forms/Photo Restrictions	___ Image Requests	___ Storage Needs

 Operations/Finance:

___ Outside Consultant Contract	___ Budget	___ Fundraising
___ Additional Security	___ Other Administrative Needs	

 Security/Docent Participation:

___ Object requirements	___ Installation requirements	___ Training

 Publications and Products:

___ Publication	___ Signage	___ Merchandise

Programs/ Education:

___ Symposium	___ Lecture(s)	___ Gallery Talk(s)
___ Teacher Resources	___ Teacher Workshops	___ Docent Training

 Operations/Finance:

___ Outside Consultant Contract	___ Budget	___ Fundraising
___ Additional Security	___ Other Administrative Needs	

 Marketing:

___ Printed Announcements	___ Invitations	___ Social Media

Events:

___ Members Event	___ Opening Dinner/Reception	___ Gala
___ Concerts	___ Other (please describe)	

Operations/Finance:
___ Outside Consultant Contract   ___ Budget   ___ Fundraising
___ Additional Security   ___ Other Administrative Needs

Marketing:
___ Printed Announcements   ___ Press Release   ___ Social Media

Capital Project:
___ Land   ___ Main Structure   ___ Other:
___ Survey/Comprehensive   ___ Building   ___ Restoration/Other:

Operations/Finance:
___ Outside Consultant Contract   ___ Budget   ___ Fundraising
___ Additional Security   ___ Other Administrative Needs

Preparation Schedule:

Date: **Activity:**

Please attach any additional information as necessary.

Approved by:

_____
Executive Director   Date

_____
Board Treasurer   Date

_____
Board President   Date

shared with the board finance committee. On an annual basis, the operating budget originates with the department heads, who submit budget requests, the contents of which are compared to income projects from the accounting staff. The annual budget is tentatively approved by the finance committee and presented to the board by the finance committee for approval by board vote.

The $1.1 million operating budget accommodates a staff of nineteen staff members, and the operation is in a period of intense growth. Contributed income is generated from corporate and individual memberships and an annual appeal, though Bones admits the energy expended in garnering contributions is relatively minimal. Instead, the mansion staff is reacting to the current boom in tourism activity in Portland by catering to visitors with enhanced tour and educational experiences. Furthermore, Bones explains that she was interested in stabilizing visitation throughout the year, rather than receiving the majority of visitors around the end-of-year holiday season, when unpredictable weather can cause closures and negatively impact revenue projections. The focus on the visitor experience and its stabilization throughout the year is twofold. From a programmatic perspective, the augmentation of tours and educational offerings with topics of public interest and general regional history broadens the narrative of the site beyond the Pittock Family History. In terms of fundraising, Bones explains that the concentration of programming is a strategic investment that creates a community based around the mansion and its activities, which will ultimately result in an expanded and committed donor base.

What can we learn?

- Whenever possible, invest in professional development and training for staff members, especially as needed to implement strategic planning. Bones says of her training: "it was great because it taught me about basic accounting, which I now understand conceptually. . . . Accounting is not black and white, but open to interpretation."
- Be flexible to market trends and how that can shift or drive operational activity. High tourism figures are causing a

boom in attendance at the mansion, and the mansion is capitalizing on the resource of visitors with a goal to future funding. Responsiveness to market changes can define your success.

*   *   *

Conclusion

This chapter has provided the final pieces to understanding your site's finances, reporting to external agencies and the IRS, and planning for the future. The act of annual reporting is not an autonomous process but is reflective of the work of the organization and its priorities, and serves to document the mission of the site as the locus of all operations. Embrace the act of forecasting to best manage your finances throughout the year, and take advantage of the Form 990 process to analyze and evaluate your organization as a charitable, mission-based organization held in and accountable to the public trust.

Key Points: Checklist

- Financial Reporting and Forecasting
  - Internal Reporting
    - Formalize Reporting Structure and Schedule
    - Monthly Financial Activity Reports
    - Quarterly Financial Reports (Budget vs. Actual vs. Forecast)
    - Fundraising Planning Worksheet
  - External Reporting
    - Grant Stewardship
    - Project Stewardship to Funders
    - Annual Report
  - Annual 990 Filing to IRS
    - Coordination with Tax Professional
    - Begin Process Six Months in Advance
    - Determine Filing Status
      - 990-N Electronic Postcard

- 990EZ
- 990
- Complete 990
  - Form 990 Completion, Including Schedules
  - Executive or Review with Tax Professional
  - Review Completed 990 with Board and Staff

Notes

1. See Richard F. Wacht, *Financial Management in Nonprofit Organizations* (Atlanta: Georgia State University Business Press, 1991), 169–74.

2. Interview with Rowena Dasch, Executive Director.

3. Colonial Dames of America in the State of Texas, http://www.nch museum.org.

4. Rowena Dasch, personal communication, February 28, 2017.

5. Internal Revenue Service, "Form 990: Return of Organization Exempt from Income Tax," Washington, D.C.: Department of the Treasury, 2016.

6. Peter Swords, "How to Read the New IRS Form 990," Accessed February 13, 2016, https://d2oc0ihd6a5bt.cloudfront.net/wp-content/uploads/sites/1482/2016/01/Chapter_1.pdf.

7. Ibid., 6.

8. For a discussion of independent contractors versus employees, see Ethan S. Klepetar, "Employee and Independent Contractor Issues in the Museum Context" in *The Legal Guide for Museum Professionals*, ed. Julia Courtney (Lanham, MD: Rowman & Littlefield, 2015).

9. Interview with Marta Bones, Executive Director.

10. Marta Bones, personal communication, March 7, 2017.

6

Conclusion

So. Here we find ourselves, at another turning point in the management of your site. You are no longer a novice, and your commitment to proper oversight has taken your site from an old building to a designated, functioning house museum. At this point, you are armed with the knowledge to foster the initial organizational phase of a site and are ready to cross the threshold to new goals in the sustenance of your site.

This book has either introduced you to new concepts, or enhanced previous knowledge you may have brought to the table. Chapter 1 took an in-depth look at the structural organization and incorporation of a historic site. We attended to issues of legal incorporation, tax exemption, and historic designation. Concepts of the business plan, the strategic plan, and the mission were addressed, all with the goal of the collective understanding between the various individuals involved in the inception of the site in regard to organizational direction and priorities. Chapter 1 guided you through the transition from a preservation enthusiast to a strategically minded site leader, able to set organizational goals and structure the essential work of the site.

Chapter 2 offered a discussion of contributed income and strategic donor engagement. Productive planning, such as community research and an understanding of your potential donor base, is essential to an effective development system. From the creation of a board development committee to a compliant gift acknowledgment structure, it is important to solicit, process, and acknowledge gifts according to coordinated and tactical efforts. We concluded chapter 2 with a description of the various categories of contribution income, including planned gifts, grants, corporate sponsorships, and nonmonetary tangible and in-kind gifts.

The focus of chapter 3 was on earned revenue, commonly understood to be money sourced from the sale of goods or services. We highlighted the need for audience evaluation and the assessment of your existing resources, and specified a number of avenues by which money can be earned, including admission fees, sale of goods, private event rentals, ticketed events, and research services, though there may be many more opportunities available at your site and in your regional market. With proper planning *and* keen evaluation, you can ensure efficient and cost-effective means by which to transition visitors to clients and customers.

Chapter 4 tackled the basic concepts of financial tracking and oversight. Topics included the formalization of systematic organizational financial management, the determination and tracking of financial sources and expenses in an operating budget, and the review of financial activity at regular intervals. The three major financial documents are the statement of financial activity, the statement of financial position, and the statement of cash flows, which were each introduced and described.

In chapter 5, we explored further the subject of financial reporting in the quarterly and annual reporting structures. We linked the concepts of financial documentation introduced in chapter 4 with forecasting, the predictive measure of tracking, analyzing, and revising income and expense expectations according to real activity. The chapter also addressed the IRS Form 990 in detail, and provided general instruction on how to understand the questions asked and how to ensure accuracy. Finally, we linked the activities of annual reporting, forecasting, and Form 990 submission with strategic short- and long-term planning for the next fiscal cycle and beyond.

Each chapter, in addition to its main topical focus, includes two case studies that illustrate the concepts in action. The case studies represent sites of a variety of organizational sizes, budgets, and staff sizes, are located across the United States, and all are at different stages in their evolution. Every site administrator quoted in this text—and countless more with whom I have spoken over the years—has faced challenges and enjoyed triumphs, tackled frustrations and relished success. While each site has a unique personality, never make the assumption that your lot is worse than the challenges faced by any of your peers and colleagues. Museum workers, and particularly historic site administrators, are resourceful, and wear their battle scars with pride. Hopefully the ten stories shared in this text put your own challenges in perspective and encourage you to persevere when faced with hard situations.

Throughout this book and illuminated within the chapters is the idea that *financial management is rhythmic*. The conclusion of one financial cycle informs the next cycle, and not simply in terms of the net assets at the end of the year. Financial planning informs and even dictates activities, including strategic planning, programs, and contributed and earned income goals. No single program or any financial goal exists in a vacuum. Instead, all operations exist in orbit around one all-encompassing message: your mission. Investment in planning and evaluation, as well as the ability to amend activities based on market needs, leads to a strong public message, which benefits your organization in terms of higher income and audience engagement. Focus on your mission, strategic planning, and mindful financial management will help to ensure that your operation exists. Historic sites that keep these priorities front and center are those that have the highest chance of remaining open for generations.

The story of your site is at the heart of your work, a concept introduced in the opening pages of this book. This story is one that continues to grow and can be shared in a variety of ways. When you applied for a historic designation, you documented the historical significance of your site. Every activity you undertake, from leading tours to sending annual appeal letters, tells your story, both the past of your site and the ways in which it is still changing. And even when you draft an operating budget or complete a Form 990, your story is told in every expense line, in the activities you offer, in the mission you support. The financial work and associated documentation of a site is a lasting record of its history.

This text is designed to walk you through many of the legal and financial situations faced in the first year of operation. You may, in fact, now find yourself to be in a different position, in which your goal is not to establish a site but to sustain the organization. Board members, staff members, and volunteers all have unique experiences and opportunities in the first year of a site's operation, and your collective knowledge will only expand. As your operation matures and grows, don't forget to keep learning. There are fantastic resources in the field of museums studies that are applicable to historic house museums and other historic sites that can help inform your future endeavors. Professional organizations are invaluable platforms for discussion and professional engagement. Consider participation in the American Alliance of Museums (AAM), which offers guidance on best practices and professional standards. You may wish to consider taking part in an AAM Museum Assessment Program (MAP), which is geared toward providing assistance to small museums in order to strengthen their administrations and plan for the future. The American Association for State and Local History (AASLH) provides pertinent material to guide you in the management of a historic site, with robust professional development resources and an active network of professionals, particularly in historic sites. Similar to MAP, AASLH also offers the Standards and Excellence Program for History Organizations (StEPS), which is particular to small or mid-sized history organizations and provides resources to help even the smallest sites evaluate their policies and practices. Together MAP and StEPs are valuable tools to assess your site and make it sustainable.

As you enter the next phase of organizational growth or simply seek additional resources that are not necessarily specific to historic sites, there are a number of texts that can provide extremely useful information for the museum field in general. *Organizing Your Museum: The Essentials* (1989), edited by Sara Dubberly, is a similar text regarding the establishment of a museum and steps to consider as you organize. Hugh H. Genoways and Lynne M. Ireland's *Museum Administration 2.0* (revised 2017) details general operations such as human resources, collections, and strategic planning. The six-volume *Small Museum Toolkit* series (2011) by Cinnamon Catlin-Legutko is also a great reference regarding the concentrated areas of governance, finance, personnel, community engagement, exhibitions, and stewardship.

I recommend other texts, particularly on law and finance, as you build your reference library. *Slaying the Financial Dragon: Strategies for Museums* (2003) offers case studies with perspective on various museums' financial situations. *To Give and To Receive: A Handbook on Gifts and Donations for Museums and Donors* (2011), edited by Sharon Smith Theobald and Laurette E. McCarthy, is a worthwhile guide to the donation process, including overviews of donor relations, valuation considerations, and tax incentives. And *The Budget-Building Book for Nonprofits: A Step-by-Step Guide for Managers and Boards* (1998) by Murray Dropkin and Bill LaTouche may not be specific to the museum field, but is an effective resource for budget planning and management. We are in a virtual Renaissance of books dedicated to the topic of museum law: Julia Courtney's *The Legal Guide for Museum Professionals* (2015), Thomas F. King's *Cultural Resource Laws and Practice* (2013), Heather Hope Kuruvilla's *A Legal Dictionary for Museum Professionals* (2016), and Marilyn E. Phelan's *Museum Law: A Guide for Officers, Directors, and Counsel* (2014) are all practical contributions to the field.

I encourage you to consider this book as the beginning of a conversation that is to be continued. As many questions that I hope have been answered within these pages, many more may have arisen. As you have established your organization, implemented priorities and systems to enact them, and tackled procedures for the first time, unforeseen situations may have left you flummoxed and left certain questions unanswered. This is exactly where you want to be right now! Your questions prove that you are still receiving information. As your organization matures, so does your knowledge base. Further, the more questions you raise and issues you tackle, the more your experience grows.

Now you're on the other side of the divide between patron and professional. You take your knowledge with you every time you set foot in a museum, and your background informs how you experience your own site and how you visit other museums. When you visit a site and feel those creaky floorboards shift under your weight, your perspective is different. You read the mission statement with an eye to strategy, you examine the admission fee structures, and you consider the aptitude of the space for private rentals. You understand the life cycle of the house to be not limited to its life in the past but also as a site alive and for the public. You know all too well how the investment of many keeps the doors open. The experience you have gained by way of incorporating a site, bringing in contributed and earned income, and managing its finances have not always been fun, but you recognize their necessity in order to create a vibrant, welcoming site. You have augmented your passion for history and museums with knowledge and with practice. You are no longer just a museum visitor. You are a contributor to the field. You have the power to make history come alive, just as others did for you when they inspired you to take that first step to save a site. Make it happen.

Glossary

Articles of Incorporation The formal declaration of organization; also referred to as "articles of association," "certificate of association," or a similar name determined by state.

Business Plan The "who and what" of your operation; the functional process by which you expect to accomplish your goals.

Bylaws A document that articulates the rules, policies, and procedures of the organization, particularly in regard to governance.

Contributed Income Revenue received from donations with no products or services provided in exchange for the funds.

Designation The status conferred to a site by a local, state, or federal agency that oversees preservation initiatives and documents sites of significance.

Earned Income Revenue generated from the sale of goods, services rendered, or work performed.

Endowment A fund of invested capital from which funds are regular distributed (usually less than the income earned).

Forecast A prediction or estimate for financial purposes.

In-Kind Donation Donations that are not monetary but are gifts of time, products, and services.

Memorandum of Understanding A document that formalizes the relationship and mutual expectations between a parent organization and a site.

Mission Statement A summary statement of the purpose, function, and goals of an organization.

Securities Gifts A form of a noncash contribution, usually of appreciated stock or mutual funds.

Spending Policy A usage structure determined by a board to ensure that the growth of the fund's assets will meet or exceed inflation over time.

Statement of Cash Flows The financial document that accounts for the change in cash and cash equivalents during a financial period, and summarizes the sources and uses of cash during the corresponding period of the statement of activity.

Statement of Financial Activity The document showing the income and the expenditures of an organization and how they relate to each other. Also called an income statement or a profit and loss statement (P&L).

Statement of Financial Position A comprehensive record of organizational financial standing. Also called a balance sheet.

Statement of Values The statement of core beliefs guiding operational activities.

Strategic Plan The "how and when" of your organization, including operation, its priorities, and goals.

Tangible Donation Donations that are not monetary but are gifts of goods, either for operational use, sale, or objects intended for interpretive use.

Vision Statement The statement of objectives and their relation to organizational potential.

Index

Page references for figures are italicized.

About the Author

Rebekah Beaulieu has been a museum professional for almost twenty years, with experience in civic museums, academic museums, and historic sites. She currently works as the associate director at the Bowdoin College Museum of Art, where she is responsible for all financial oversight, risk management, and administration of the museum. She previously served as the inaugural executive director of the Winchester Historical Society and the Sanborn House Historical and Cultural Center in Winchester, Massachusetts. Rebekah has extensive experience in nonprofit financial management, fundraising, and board relations and has presented workshops on grant writing, budget management, and fiscal sustainability in historic sites.

In addition to her professional experience, Beaulieu holds a BA in American Studies and Art History from George Washington University, an MA in Art History and Museum Studies from the University of Wisconsin–Milwaukee, an MA in Arts Administration from Columbia University, and a PhD in American and New England Studies from Boston University. She has presented research at the meetings of organizations such as the Society of American City and Regional Planning, the Popular/American Culture Association, the College Art Association, and the National Council for Public History.

Beaulieu is a board member of the New England Museum Association and active in the American Alliance of Museums as a certified Accreditation/MAP Peer Reviewer. She also serves as a trustee of the Pejepscot Historical Society and a member of the Village Review Board in Brunswick, Maine.

Visit her website at www.museummaverick.com or contact her directly at rebekah.beaulieu@gmail.com.